THE RIVERTON RIFLE

The Riverton Rifle

Straight Shooting on Hockey and on Life

My Story

Reggie Leach

with **Randi Druzin**

Foreword by **Bobby Clarke**

GREYSTONE BOOKS

Vancouver/Berkeley

15 16 17 18 19 5 4 3 2 1

Greystone Books Ltd.
www.greystonebooks.com

Cataloguing data available from Library and Archives Canada
isbn 978-1-77164-137-1 (cloth)
isbn 978-1-77164-138-8 (epub)

Editing by Jennifer Croll
Proofreading by Stephanie Fysh
Jacket design by Peter Cocking
Text design by Nayeli Jimenez
Photographs provided by Reggie Leach
Printed and bound in Canada by Friesens
Distributed in the U.S. by Publishers Group West

We gratefully acknowledge the financial support of the Canada Council for the Arts, the British Columbia Arts Council, the Province of British Columbia through the Book Publishing Tax Credit, and the Government of Canada through the Canada Book Fund for our publishing activities.

Greystone Books is committed to reducing the consumption of old-growth forests in the books it publishes. This book is one step towards that goal.

For my grandchildren, Jaden, Hunter, and Jaxon: you're the future, and the reason why I wrote this book.

And for all the young people who struggle in life: I hope my story can help you make good choices and overcome the challenges that may come your way.

Table of Contents

Foreword

BY BOBBY CLARKE

I MET REGGIE IN the summer of 1966, a few weeks before the start of the Flin Flon Bombers training camp. When I walked into the Whitney Forum that day, I saw a big kid standing on the concrete in the middle of the rink firing pucks at the net. We chatted for a few minutes and hit it off right away. We became fast friends and by the time our rookie season was a few months old, we were inseparable.

We jelled as linemates, too. I would feed him in the puck in the slot, knowing that he would unleash a killer shot. It was powerful and accurate enough to terrify goalies, first in Junior A and then in the NHL. He was stronger and faster than most of us, but it wasn't his natural gifts alone that accounted for his phenomenal success as a goal-scorer. Reggie spent hours on end working on his shot.

He showed that same determination in rebuilding his life after alcohol almost destroyed it. He went to rehab and, though he faced some big challenges in the years that followed, he never once turned to alcohol to help him cope. Instead, he built a successful landscaping business, strengthened ties to family members and friends, and formed new relationships. He also dedicated himself to helping others and to improving the lives of First Nations people. His rebirth is truly inspirational. Reggie impresses me more now than he ever has. I'm proud to call him my former teammate, my friend, and even my brother.

1

Riverton

(1950–1966)

"The Flyers have won the second in a row. The Flyers have won their second consecutive Stanley Cup and the whole Flyers bench is on the ice!"

Philadelphia Flyers play-by-play announcer,
May 27th, 1975

MOST PEOPLE KNOW me from my playing days in Philadelphia, when the Broad Street Bullies ruled the NHL with iron fists, but my life story starts a few decades earlier and almost two thousand miles northwest, on the windswept Canadian Prairies.

My biological parents met in Winnipeg in 1949. Archie Leach, who was twenty-two when I was born, was just starting out as a blaster in mining and construction and his work took him to remote regions in the North—he went wherever he could find contracts. Jessie Ackabee, then twenty-one, was from the Eagle Lake First Nation, an Ojibwe community in Northwestern Ontario. She lived in rooming house in Winnipeg with Archie's sister, Edna, who was only nineteen.

The one small room where the two young ladies lived had no furniture aside from a cot, a sofa bed, and a tiny wooden table with two chairs. They shared a dingy bathroom with the rest of the building's residents.

The room must have seemed even smaller when I came along on April 23rd, 1950. The girls were struggling to make ends meet at the time, and even with Archie sending money whenever he could, they didn't have enough to provide for themselves and me.

Edna suggested they leave me in the care of her parents, who lived in Riverton, a small community seventy miles north of Winnipeg. Jessie was faced with an agonizing decision. She didn't want to part with me, but she knew my paternal grandparents could provide me with a better life, so she agreed to the arrangement. She viewed it as temporary and hoped to be reunited with me down the road, when she was able to care for me.

When I was a few weeks old, Edna bundled me up and we boarded a train to Riverton, where my paternal grandparents would raise me. Edna said I didn't fuss at all and seemed to enjoy the regular swaying of the passenger car—a good sign, I guess, for someone who would later spend much of his working life on the road.

RIVERTON WAS A small, bustling community on the western shore of Lake Winnipeg. It was the last stop on the Canadian Pacific rail line extending north from Winnipeg, so it had a steady stream of goods moving in and out of town. Fishermen would arrive with their haul of goldeye and whitefish while gold extracted from the soil sixty miles east across lake Winnipeg was being loaded onto boxcars. Most of the nine hundred people who lived in the community were of Icelandic or Ukrainian descent. There were some First Nation families too.

On the sunny May afternoon that I arrived, my grandfather headed to the train station telling people he was about to pick up a "special delivery." He beamed when Edna clambered off the train and handed me to him. Edna noticed some raised eyebrows when she looked around the platform; unwed mothers weren't exactly celebrated in those days. But she was a plucky girl and she wasted no time in assuring bystanders that I was not her child. They didn't believe her, but she just shrugged and headed to her parents' home to celebrate my arrival. My grandfather was so proud that day, he gave me his name—Reginald Joseph Leach.

AFTER COMPLETING MILITARY service in his native England, my grandfather had moved to Canada and found work at Favourable Lake Mine in Northern Ontario. That is where he met Kate McKay, who had grown up on the Berens River First Nation, a small Ojibwe community accessible only by boat on the eastern shore of Lake Winnipeg. Kate and my grandfather Reginald were likely introduced by my great-uncle, Brother Frederick Leach, who served at the Catholic Mission in Berens River and wrote a book titled *60 Years with Indians and Settlers on Lake Winnipeg*. He loved living among the Ojibwe and Saulteax people of the region and became an advocate for their way of living. I remember meeting him once as a child when he visited my grandfather.

The couple got married and started a family in the Favourable Lake region of Northwestern Ontario long before they relocated to Riverton, where my grandfather took a job managing a freight house owned by the Berens River Mining Company. They had Archie, Edna, and ten other children: Alfred, Anthony, Cyril, Constance, Kathy, Richard, Dorothy, Rudy, Evelyn, and Joyce. A few years after I arrived, my grandparents also adopted my cousin, Karen. Raising fourteen kids could not have been easy for Reginald and Kate.

My grandparents embraced me from the start, calling me "Little Reggie," and raised me as their own son. To this day, I refer to them as my parents and I think of their children as my siblings, though most of them had already moved out with careers of their own by the time I arrived.

Archie would visit now and then, sometimes with his buddies from the mines. To me he was just another older sibling who came home for a few days at a time. I was always excited when one of my brothers would come home and tell stories about their travels. They often brought friends with them, too. Archie and I would chat a little and then I would be on my way out the door to play with my friends. I found out he was my biological father when I was about eleven years old, but it didn't faze me much. I was a happy kid. It seems that Archie was popular with the ladies. A few years ago, a woman approached me at a shopping mall and told me she had once dated him. It was clear from her enthusiasm and the way she swooned over him that the tall, thin, and handsome man had made quite an impression on her.

There were drawbacks to being the baby in such a large family. I was always pestering my siblings, hoping to be included in their activities. To get me out of the way, my brothers would prop me on top of a fence post in our front yard and leave me there. I probably could have climbed down, but four feet seems like a big drop when you're a kid. When I finally did muster the courage to take the leap, I was surprised and quite happy to have survived.

We lived in a small, sparsely furnished, wood-frame house on a back street near the center of town. We only had the basic necessities in our home, nothing fancy. It had a long hallway along one side of the building that connected a front room, which served as a living room and a sleeping area for my mom and dad, one middle bedroom with three bunk beds for us kids, and a small kitchen with a wood cook stove at the back. Our home always had that warm smell of wood. We had no indoor plumbing. The only kind of running water we had was me running to haul the water. We used water from an artesian well near the center of town for drinking, cooking, and washing. I claimed a small closet as my bedroom. I slept on a nest I built on the floor from a pile of clothes and found it comfortable—I kid you not. I considered it the best room in the house. Our home seemed so safe and comfortable to me even though we didn't own much. And growing up, I never, ever saw my parents drink alcohol.

MY MOTHER WAS a quiet woman who didn't speak much unless she had something important to say. She made do with a very limited budget to feed us all. Many of our meals consisted of potatoes from her small garden, macaroni, homemade bread, and whatever meat was affordable at the time—we ate a lot of bologna. She was also a kind and generous person who repaired clothes for people and would often mend socks for local hockey teams. I have a vivid memory of her repairing the upholstery of a friend's car. She did all these things for just a few bucks, next to nothing. She also loved Halloween and would spend a week making fudge bars to hand out to the two hundred or so kids in Riverton. I think that's why I go overboard on decorations for Halloween and making it fun for the kids these days, like she did. She also made and sold beaded moccasins to bring in some money. I would help her sort the beads by color, spending hours separating them into little piles.

She was always there when I needed her. One winter, when I was about six or seven, I managed to get my tongue stuck to the blade of an axe. At that age, the axe was bigger than me! I don't remember how I managed to get in that predicament, but I do remember crawling into the house in a panic, dragging the axe along the ground. My mother used some warm water to free me. I don't remember her reaction—she probably just laughed—but I remember it hurt like heck.

My mother never lost her temper with me either, except on one memorable occasion. Like a lot of kids, I hated bedtime. Determined to stay awake one night, I tried to turn on the light, which was just above the small potbelly wood stove that heated the bedroom and the rest of our house. I took a tumble and severely burned the outside of my arm from my elbow to my wrist. I didn't say anything because I was afraid of getting in trouble, but my teacher noticed the burn the next day and sent me home. My mother was upset that I hadn't told her what happened and she gave me a serious tongue-lashing.

She also scolded me for being greedy one Christmas when I received two cowboy gun holsters from my sisters. One was brown and the other one was black with studs. The studded one was pretty sharp. I refused to share either with Rudy, who was a few years older than me, even though we were close—I followed him around like a puppy in those days. My mother insisted I hand one over, emphasizing the importance of sharing, which was an important life lesson. I did as I was told but kept the studded one.

I also had a good relationship with my father. He was strict but he was full of life and he could be very playful. I used to taunt him by repeating those lines from Jack and the Beanstalk: "Fee-fi-fo-fum, I smell the blood of an Englishman!" He would chase me around the house for that but I don't think he ever caught me.

When I was about seven years old, he contracted tuberculosis and spent two years in a sanatorium in Winnipeg. He wasn't strong enough to work after that so my parents and the five kids who were still living at home survived on social assistance. We always seemed to have food, but nothing fancy. My father spent most of his time in the house, reading or working on those paint-by-number pictures. Every now and then, he would venture out to the pool hall and take me with him.

The hall was a single-story box-style wood structure. In addition to a handful of pool tables, it had a barber's chair, a tuck shop, and tiny living quarters. I was six years old the first time I went there. I was a few inches shorter than the table so I had to stand on a box to see. Someone hit a ball that jumped up and hit me smack in the face—my first of many black eyes.

My father was pretty slick with the cue. The "Silver Fox" taught me the fundamentals of the game. The owner, Casper Smigelski, also gave me some tips over the next few years. He would let me play for free in exchange for doing chores like cleaning the tables and taking out the garbage. More than once, I climbed into that barber's chair and he cut my hair. I was a pretty good pool player by the time I was a teenager, and that served me well later in life.

Not too far from the pool hall was the town's one and only movie theater. A ticket for the show was just a quarter, so I managed to go once in a while. The day I saw an Elvis Presley movie, I went to bed puzzled, scratching my head. I couldn't figure out how he could be on the silver screen and singing on the radio in my grandparents' home moments later. We didn't have a television at home when I was growing up, so the magic of film was a foreign concept to me.

THERE'S A WELL-KNOWN saying that it takes a village to raise a child, and I couldn't agree more. Looking back at my earliest years, I see dozens of friends and neighbors who played a pivotal role in my life. I guess you could say the town of Riverton raised me. Over my life I had several great father figures, and many were in Riverton.

A businessman named Paul Luprypa was one of the many locals who helped me in some way. In addition to owning the movie theater, he also owned a general store. He didn't really need my help but he gave me odd jobs to do, knowing that the few bucks I earned would help out my family. I spent a lot of time at the store, which doubled as a showroom for farming implements, hauling wood, and delivering fuel to farmers along with Paul's sons, Eddy and Freddy.

Paul's wife would make sandwiches for us to eat on those runs to the countryside. I was overwhelmed the first time I bit into a ham and cheese sandwich. It tasted like a gourmet meal to me. Deli meat was a luxury my family couldn't afford.

The Luprypa brothers and I would also unload supplies from the trucks that pulled up to the store. I tried to roll a twenty-gallon oil drum off a truck early one summer, but I was about nine years old and not nearly strong enough. I didn't succeed, but I swore I would be able to move that thing by the end of the summer—and I did. When I set a goal for myself, I work to achieve it.

Freddy, the younger of the Luprypa brothers, was about six years older than me but we became inseparable despite the age difference. He taught me how to drive by putting me behind the wheel of his family's half-ton international truck when I was barely tall enough to reach the pedals. I managed to stay out of the ditch, but looking back, I have no idea how.

When I was a bit older, I helped the Luprypa family build a nine-hole golf course in Arnes, a tiny community south of

“Reggie was just a little fellow and he spent a lot of time working with us. We taught him to work the lawn mower and drive a tractor. I once put him behind the wheel of a truck that I was towing. He was able to start the engine but he had a tough time controlling the vehicle. When I stopped, he tried to do the same. Unfortunately, he couldn’t reach the brakes. He ended up ramming into my truck and smashing the taillight. It wasn’t a big deal because the light wasn’t working anyway. I guess Reggie was just too small to be doing what he was doing.”

ED LUPRYPA

Riverton. I used to drive a little tractor around the place, on the hunt for boulders and stones that needed to be removed. Eddy, Freddy, and I helped maintain the course after it opened. I seeded grass, laid sod, and trimmed trees and shrubs. I also cut the greens and fairways. All this knowledge came in handy after I retired from hockey, but I'll get to that later.

Freddy and I remained close for decades. When I turned pro, our families would spend summers together in and around Arnes. Freddy never saw me play hockey except on television, but he followed my career closely. I was delighted when he and his wife, Ladine, showed up for my induction into the Manitoba Sports Hall of Fame in 1997.

Freddy said "goodbye" when we parted ways at the end of that night. It struck me as odd; he had once told me you should never say "goodbye'" because it's so final. He preferred "see you later." Well, Freddy and I never saw each other after that day. He died in his sleep the following year and his passing left a big void in my life.

AS A YOUNGSTER, when I wasn't working at the golf course in the summer, I was playing baseball or road hockey. There were a lot of kids in town, so when we played, we divided ourselves into four teams, one from each quadrant of the town. The teams squared off against each other out front of the hotel, which was adjacent to the pool hall and looked just like it except that it had two floors. I was a goalie back then because I was too short and chubby to be anything else. We played for hours on end.

We played road hockey in the winter too, when the mercury plunged to −14°F and our clothes were so bulky they weighed almost as much as we did. We made goalposts out of ice and that worked out well for the most part, but there was one problem: every hour or so a truck would drive by and crush the posts. We had no choice but to put the game on hold to make new ones. Other times, when I could borrow a pair of skates, my friends and I would skate on the ice in the frozen ditches that lined the roads around town. We had a lot of fun doing that.

Of course, we spent a lot of time in school too. I wasn't interested in academics at all—I had to repeat Grade 1—and I was always in trouble. Two buddies and I were once thrown out of class and ordered to sit in the cloakroom, where our classmates kept their lunches. The three of us proceeded to eat all the food in that room. The farm kids had the best lunches; their satchels were stuffed with big sandwiches, fresh fruit, and homemade cakes and pies. It was a treat for me, but those hijinks landed me in hot water.

I was punished so often, the strap became like an old friend. One school year, I got the strap about ten times. It hurt to be thrashed with a leather belt, but it probably did more damage to my ego. I just held my hands out and took my punishment with a grin, trying hard to pretend it didn't hurt—and I went right on misbehaving. I would sometimes get to school early to hide the strap from our teachers. I had a small problem with authority, even then. A buddy and I once I held a competition to see who could get the strap the most times in one school year. I think I won.

When I was thirteen years old, I had a serious altercation with a teacher who seemed to have it in for one of the smallest kids in class. One day, the teacher grabbed the boy by his ear and twisted it until the kid was crying in pain. I asked the teacher to stop but he just twisted harder—so I pushed him away. He was being a bully and it bothered me. It may be a funny thing for me to say given that I later played for the Broad

Street Bullies, but there you have it. I have always felt the need to stand up for the underdog. I got suspended for a week. Years later, that kid became a successful businessman and he went out of his way to thank me for sticking up for him.

The one thing I liked about school, and excelled at, was organized sports. I ran track and played on the baseball team. I was a big, strong kid by the time I was in Grade 5, so I was a power hitter. I loved playing catcher because it meant I could be part of the action without having to run all over the place. Most people don't know that I was born with poor eyesight in my left eye. It probably could have been corrected with glasses early on, but we couldn't afford them so I learned to compensate. It didn't seem to interfere with my ability to play sports. It really should have made playing right wing more difficult, but for some reason, it didn't.

I FOLLOWED THE NHL, listening to radio broadcasts of the games with my father, who was a big sports fan. I idolized Gordie Howe. All the kids in town knew "Mr. Hockey," not just because he was an NHL star but also because he was a fixture in advertisements in the department store catalogues. I met Gordie many years later and discovered he was a mere mortal, but when I was a kid, I thought of him as a superhero. Actually, I still think of him as a superhero!

I didn't put on skates until I was ten years old. The first pair I tried on had belonged to one of my brothers and was about twice as big as my feet. I had to stuff them with newspapers so I could use them. They were uncomfortable, but that didn't dampen my enthusiasm for hockey. I loved the sport from the start and I excelled at it. Before long, I was playing on teams in several age groups, still using borrowed skates and hand-me-downs.

I was on the ice at the Riverton Memorial Arena playing hockey about five days a week, but I wanted to be out there every day of the week, so I also signed up for figure skating and joined the girls on Wednesdays and Saturdays. I took part in some figure skating carnivals—no word of a lie. I loved being on the ice in front of a crowd, showing off my bunny hop jump or camel spin. I'm certain those lessons helped make me a strong skater.

But even that wasn't enough ice time for me. After the arena closed for the night, I would sneak into the building, which was essentially a barn, and spend hours on the ice by myself, skating in circles and firing pucks at the net. I would pick a target and shoot at it until I hit it, again and again. In time, I could fire the puck from the top of the face-off circle and hit the exact spot where the crossbar and the post intersected. The arena was completely dark at that hour except for the beams of moonlight that shone through knotholes in the slats of wood. Most people in town knew that I was there because they could hear the puck ringing off the crossbar in the middle of the night. It didn't seem to bother them because no one ever asked me to leave. I guess they figured no harm was being done.

Of course, I wasn't the only one who spent a lot of time in that building. The arena is the center of community life in many Canadian towns, and that was certainly true in Riverton. It was a beehive of activity with people either on the ice—curling, figure skating, or playing hockey—or watching from the sidelines. The ice was packed during recreational skating hours and I spent that time weaving in and out of traffic, playing tag with my buddies. When I wasn't on the ice, I was running along the outside of the boards and climbing over the benches hunting for stray pucks.

When our family moved into a bigger home, I created a small patch of ice in the backyard by hauling buckets of water from an outside well. I spent two or three hours at a time shooting the puck at a plywood board propped up against the shed. I had marked targets on the wood to shoot at. I was determined to have the best shot around. Friends would sometimes join me out there and we held friendly competitions.

OUR FAMILY MOVED into that home when I was about twelve years old. It was a small stucco structure, but it felt like a mansion to me. It still didn't have indoor plumbing, but it had three bedrooms, a living room, and a decent-sized kitchen. It was a lot more living space than I was used to. For the first time in my life, I had my own bed. I slept in the shed in the summer, mainly so that I could slip away at night without my mother knowing about it. I rarely escaped detection, though; she had a clear view of the shed from her bedroom window.

Around that time, my brother Richard was in an accident. He wrapped his car around a telephone pole and passed away. Although he was almost a decade older than me and was living in Selkirk, Manitoba, with his wife and two kids, the news sure threw me for a loop. I still remember the funeral and seeing him lying in that casket. It was the first time I had ever seen a dead body and experienced that kind of loss. Our family was devastated.

A couple of months after that, my parents went out to play bingo one night and I stayed home to watch a CFL game between the Edmonton Eskimos and the Winnipeg Blue Bombers. I was thrilled when the Eskimos won because it meant I had finally won a bet with my father. I was looking forward to collecting my nickel from him, but my mother came home alone with some horrible news. My father had died of a heart attack. I ran across town to find my sister Evelyn, who was just a few years older than me. Neither of us knew what to do. For a long time after my father died, the house seemed empty no matter how many people were in it. I really missed him.

Three months later, Evelyn and her boyfriend drove to a secluded spot and parked there. They were teenagers, after all. They fell asleep while the motor was running and died of carbon monoxide poisoning. I was at home watching coverage of the assassination of U.S. President John F. Kennedy when a family friend came to our door to deliver the news. Evelyn and I had grown up together and we had always been close. Losing her was a huge blow. From then on, my mother, Karen, and I were the only three people living in the house.

One of the people who helped us through this difficult time was my older sister Dorothy. Even though she lived and worked in Winnipeg, she came home almost every weekend, partially to visit the man who became her husband, Buddy, but also to support us. She became my touchstone. She was someone I could talk to, who listened to me and was always in my corner. We became closer when I started playing pro hockey and I would call her often, just to check up on the family. She helped me through the low times, but she has been by my side through many good times too. Both she and Buddy are very special to me to this day.

Even though we were surrounded by love and support, the loss of three close family members within a few short months was a terrible experience for us, especially my mother—but it didn't break her. I believe she stayed strong for us, especially as our sole provider. Her friends and the good people of Riverton really supported us. She spent time with friends and continued to do the things she loved, like playing bingo, sewing for people, and cooking. Years later, I would come home during the off-season and take her to the bingo hall. She just loved it.

TO HELP ME cope, I poured myself into hockey. It kept me busy and took my mind off things. By the time I was fourteen years old, I was representing Riverton in the Bantam, Midget, and Juvenile age groups. Riverton teams were a force to be reckoned with. My bantam and midget teams won the provincial championships. My juvenile team once lost in the finals to a team from Carman, Manitoba. Its roster included two players, Brian and Chuck Lefley, who ended up in the NHL.

I eventually started suiting up for some games with the senior team, the Riverton Lions. When I was a little kid, the Lions were as big a deal to me as the Toronto Maple Leafs were to kids in Toronto. I used to make my own hockey sticks by gluing and taping together the remnants of the Lions' broken sticks. I was in awe of guys like Marvin Bjornson, Bruce Stratton, Olafur Thorsteinson, Benny Holyk, Ballan Settee, Raymond Benedictson, Harry Krueger, Brian Thorarinson, the three Johannson boys (Richie, Barry, and Doug), as well as Lloyd Roche. Lloyd could skate like the wind and I learned a lot from him.

I looked up to all the senior players, especially Joe Tergesen. He was one of the best players on the Arborg Falcons. He had played with Team Canada in 1949 and was considered a local celebrity. I used to peek around the corner on the second floor of the arena to watch him and the others eat after games. I would just stare in amazement. I could hardly believe this hockey god chewed his food like a regular person.

Before I played for the Riverton Lions I traveled to Winnipeg to watch them play a championship game in the Winnipeg

Arena. It held about ten thousand people at that time and it seemed huge to me. Years later, I would play junior hockey in that building, and I eventually played against the Winnipeg Jets.

Needless to say, I was pretty excited when I stepped on the ice for the first time wearing the Lions' red jersey. The other players were about a decade older than me, but I held my own. Before long, I was able to control the game from the blue line. I was a defenseman in those days.

I was good enough to catch the attention of a Detroit Red Wings scout named Joe Mandella, who urged me to try out for their Junior A team in Weyburn, Saskatchewan. I headed there in the fall of 1965 with two other players from Riverton, Keith Tomasson and Bobby Johannson.

The arena made an impression on me because it had indoor plumbing, not something I was used to. I was also impressed by two players there who still stand out in my mind. They were identical twins who were paired together on defense. They weren't that big but they were very tough and seemed to hit everything in sight. I don't know what became of them, but I didn't end up playing for the Weyburn Red Wings. I was the last player cut in training camp and it was a big blow because I had never had a setback in hockey up till that point.

I stopped in Winnipeg on the way home and tried out for the Winnipeg Monarchs, another Junior A team, but I got cut after my second day in camp.

That same season, Keith and I took a bus from Riverton to Lashburn, Saskatchewan, and suited up for the Junior B team. We played games on the weekend. On weekdays, I went to school and then to practice. I spent the rest of my time in the basement doing a whole lot of nothing. I was a shy kid. Keith stuck it out, but I was so homesick I came home for Christmas

“**Reggie** was a fast skater and he had a wicked shot, even then. He was also very strong. He was just a kid when he played on our senior team but he held his own, which was incredible given that it was a really rough league with players who were well into their twenties. I remember this one game in particular against a team from Stonewall, Manitoba. Reggie was behind our net with the puck when a forward from the other team, a giant, went charging in after him. We all expected Reggie to get flattened. Our goalie even skated out of the crease, ready to jump to his defense. But he didn't need to. The forward just bounced off the kid and fell to the ice. It was quite a sight!”

LLOYD ROCHE

and never went back. I spent the rest of the season playing with my old teams in Riverton. It was a mistake not to keep with it and pursue my dreams. A lot of kids still make that same kind of mistake today, likely because at home, they were treated a little like a superstar, but at a more competitive level their star doesn't shine quite as bright. So they return to where they believe they are appreciated more. But players should push themselves to more competitive levels so they can hone their skills alongside better players. Hanging in there really paid off for Keith—he was called up to the Junior A team in Weyburn before the end of the season.

I might have stayed in Riverton if not for a great man named Siggi Johnson, a local businessman whose store stocked electrical appliances. He had a big family and was very involved in minor hockey. Siggi, along with Kenny Thorsteinson, taught me a lot about hockey. Siggi was my coach for a few seasons, but he was more than that. He had also been a good friend of Archie, and he was a mentor to me.

Before I went to Weyburn, he presented me with a brand-new pair of CCM Tacks skates, the first pair of new skates I ever owned and the first to fit me properly. He told me it was a gift from the entire town, probably to let me know everyone there supported me, but I knew it was from him. The skates must have set him back about sixty-five dollars—a big sum back then, especially for a man with so many mouths to feed.

Just after I returned from Lashburn, Siggi took me to the local restaurant and sat me down for a heart-to-heart talk. He asked me what I wanted to do with my life and I told him I wanted to be a professional hockey player. To do that, he said, I would have to play for a high-caliber team—and that meant leaving Riverton.

To this day, I remember what happened next. He pointed to a guy on the street outside the restaurant, the local drunk, and said, "That guy was once a good hockey player, too. If you don't make a change, you're going to end up like him." No one had ever taken such an interest in my future. His words made a big impact—I was actually scared. I always respected Siggi's advice as I knew he cared.

I told him I was ready play on a top junior team, but not one that required its players go to school. I still had no interest in academics. He made some phone calls, and a few months later I was headed 450 miles north to a mining town on the Manitoba-Saskatchewan border called Flin Flon.

Deciding to leave Riverton and say goodbye to my family, neighbors, and friends was one of the hardest choices I have ever had to make. But as it turned out, it was the right move. I never lived there again but my life in Riverton and the people who made it so special—from family and friends to coaches, teammates, and even the hockey parents who made sandwiches for us—are still with me. More than fifty years later, it's still a thrill for me to visit Riverton and be welcomed by the great people there who have honored me with a street, buildings, and signs in my name.

The Bombers

(1966–1970)

I STEPPED OFF THE bus in Flin Flon on a sunny morning in May 1966 feeling a little uncertain. I was just sixteen years old, I didn't know anyone in town, and I only had seven dollars in my pocket, four of which I had borrowed. There I was, months before the actual team try-outs, all because Siggi encouraged me to make the hard choice of leaving town before I changed my mind.

I was very shy in those days, but I managed to strike up a conversation with a friendly woman named Mary Reid, who ran a restaurant at the bus depot with her husband, Jack. When I told her I was in town to try out for the Flin Flon Bombers, she said she was surprised that I was there so early, but impressed by my eagerness to join the Junior A team. The Reids were big supporters of the Bombers. Jack was on the executive board and he and Mary also ran the concession stand at the Whitney Forum.

I spent the entire day in the back corner booth of their restaurant waiting for the team's coach, Tom Baird. When he showed up after work, he wasn't sure what to do with me. It was too early in the off-season to billet me with a local family and the team couldn't cover my expenses because I hadn't yet made the roster. The Reids kindly offered to put me up for a few days until the details of my living accommodations could be worked out. Well, those few days stretched into three years. Jack and Mary welcomed me into their home and treated me like part of the family. I became close to both of them and their teenaged children, Ricky and Linda. Their kindness made a big impact on my life.

Flin Flon was a booming mining town. Most of the men worked for the Hudson Bay Mining and Smelting Company, mining the local rock for copper and zinc ore. Around 15,000 people from different ethnic backgrounds lived there. Many of the miners lived in boarding houses, so they ate most of their meals at the Reids' restaurant. Because of this, it was one of the town's most popular gathering places, and I ate most of my meals there with Jack and Mary. As a result, I got to know the regulars quite well.

The Bombers were at the center of life in the town, and every game was a social event. The arena was packed whenever the team played. Fans would take their seats at the Whitney Forum, usually the same seats for every game, as they purchased season tickets in advance, and catch up with friends and neighbors while watching the action on the ice.

The Hudson Bay Mining and Smelting Company subsidized the team and gave us jobs year-round so we could have pocket money during our playing days, while the Bombers paid for our room and board. I worked at the mines through all my years with the Bombers. At first I was a steward, doing odd jobs in the yard or maintenance work for the bosses, because I was too young to work inside the main facility. When I turned eighteen, I worked as a supervisor inside the mill, cleaning the conveyer belts and that kind of thing. During the regular season, the other players and I worked from 8 a.m. until noon then headed to the rink for our afternoon practice. During my first summer in Flin Flon, before I earned a place on the team, I worked as a carpenter's apprentice for a small construction company. That helped me pocket a little spending money, which I really appreciated. The Reids helped find that job for me, even though they refused to take anything from me for room and board. I was used to hard, physical work by then. I have never shied away from it.

AT THE END of August, I reported to training camp at the Forum. I was feeling determined. I knew I was a good hockey player who could help the team, but I wasn't sure the Bombers would feel the same way; the Weyburn Red Wings sure hadn't. I had to show them what I could do.

I was just one of many new faces in the dressing room. The Bombers had finished dead last in the Saskatchewan Junior Hockey League the previous season and management wanted to rebuild, so they invited more than seventy kids to training camp that summer. They also hired Pat Ginnell to replace Tom as coach. Paddy had played for the Bombers' Memorial Cup championship team in the 1956–57 season and spent most of the next decade playing in the minors. This was his first coaching gig.

Paddy wanted a tough team and he pushed us hard in training camp. We were on the ice four hours a day, two in the morning and two in the afternoon. We did some dryland training too. In one drill, two players would stand at either end of the blue line then sprint toward the end boards and smash into each other behind the net. I did that drill again and again. I was in a lot of pain but I never backed down.

I stood up to the veterans, too. George Forgie was a stocky, hard-nosed defenseman and one of the meanest guys in the league. He was on me all the time during camp and once shouted at me in a scrimmage for swinging my stick too high when I skated. I came close to hitting his head a few times. But I just kept doing my thing; I wanted to let him know he couldn't intimidate me. Paddy called me into his office one day and I walked in there with my stomach in knots. I was afraid he was going to send me packing as he had already done with some of the other guys. But it was good news. Paddy said I was too fast to be playing defense and he planned to move me up to right wing. He told me I would be playing on a line with a center who quite honestly looked more like a bookworm than a hockey player.

Bobby Clarke, the son of a local miner, was about the same height as me, six feet tall, but was twenty pounds lighter. He also wore dark-rimmed glasses with the short haircut we all had in those days. Clarkie was a diabetic who had to take insulin injections every day. But no two ways about it, he was a force to be reckoned with on the ice. What he lacked in natural talent he made up for with tenacity. He was always going full tilt, chasing the puck like a hound hunting a fox. In his mind, that puck was *his* puck and he wouldn't let up until he had it on his stick. At the end of every shift, he stepped off the ice drenched in sweat with his hair matted on his forehead.

He had that gap-toothed grin even then—and he wasn't alone. We didn't wear mouthguards in those days and most of us spent time at some point searching for a tooth on the ice. I lost a front tooth when someone high-sticked me. I had an implant put in, but that got knocked out too and took some of my gums with it.

Clarkie had great vision of the ice and was an incredible playmaker. He led by example and was our leader on and off the ice. He was so good I had heard about him back in Riverton. We met a few weeks after I arrived in Flin Flon when he spotted me at the arena practicing my shot. There was no ice there in the summer, so I stood on the concrete firing the puck at a net. It wasn't long before we became fast friends. We shared a great bond: our love of hockey.

BEFORE THE START of the 1966–67 Manitoba Junior Hockey League season—the Saskatchewan Junior Hockey League had folded—we were given team jerseys. We wore the same colors as our NHL sponsor, the Detroit Red Wings. I picked the red and white jersey with number 9 on the back because it was Gordie Howe's number. That jersey may have actually been worn by my hero at some point as the Red Wings often recycled their old jerseys for their junior teams. I liked to think that Howe's magic transferred to me when I donned that sweater.

From the moment the puck dropped in the first game, Clarkie and I clicked as linemates. On a typical play, Clarkie would get the puck and hold onto it until he could feed it to me coming up the right side—as a winger, I had been taught to come into the play a bit late. So then I would let 'er rip from the top of the face-off circle inside the blue line. If he couldn't get the puck to me in the high slot the first time, I would circle around and he would put it on my stick the second time. With a great hard-nosed winger named Ron Burwash playing on the left side, we became a pretty good line and teams around the league took notice.

Clarkie and I pushed each other, competed with each other in a way, and it paid off. We both had great seasons. He set league records for most goals (71), assists (112), and points (183) and was named rookie of the year. I finished third overall in goals (67) and fourth in points (113).

We shared the spotlight with some talented teammates, including Chris Worthy and Gerry Hart. Chris was one heck of a goaltender. He had been bombarded with shots the previous season but managed to post quite a few shutouts. Hart was a small defenseman but a great skater who could really move the puck. He wasn't a fighter, but he was always in somebody's face. Both those guys later turned pro.

Quite a few guys from my junior days turned pro, not just my teammates but also players from other teams. There were a lot of great young hockey players in Western Canada at the time—like Blaine Stoughton, Murray Anderson, Gene Carr, and Chuck Arnason, to name a few. Some of the guys from my junior days ended up being my teammates in Philadelphia. Dave Schultz, Don Saleski, and Orest Kindrachuk are a few who come to mind.

The Bombers weren't just talented, we were tough and nasty—just the way Paddy wanted it. We intimidated opponents the way the Broad Street Bullies did later on. Guys on other teams would often come down with "the Flin Flon flu" and sit out games against us. I got into a few fights myself and was suspended once or twice.

Our fans could be rough, too. Every now and then one of them would lean over the boards and take a swing at one of our opponents. It wasn't hard to do in those days because there was no glass around the rink, just chicken wire at either end. A few times, I looked over at the visitors' bench and saw sticks swinging and punches flying as players and spectators mixed it up. Diehard Bombers' fans would sometimes rough up our opponents after a game when the poor guys passed the stands on the long walk to the visitors' dressing room.

We finished first (42–6–0) among seven teams in the league that season. We took on the Brandon Wheat Kings in the final. They were a strong team with some big guns like Juha Widing and Billy Fairbairn, who finished just behind Clarkie in overall scoring that season. We managed to beat them three games to two. We were ecstatic and so were the fans. The Bombers had risen from the bottom to the top in less than a year and had clinched the title for the first time since 1960. The town had quite a celebration.

EVEN WHEN WE weren't playing hockey, Clarkie and I were inseparable. Some people called us the Gold Dust Twins or the Lone Ranger and Tonto. I think I was the Lone Ranger! We spent most of our downtime together and even wore some of the same clothes. If a Bomber player got a hat trick or was named star of the game, a local clothing store, Dembinsky's, would give him a gift certificate. Clarkie and I each had a few of those certificates and we used them to buy the same shirts, jackets, or pants. Not only did we dress the same, we also had the same haircuts. We shaved our heads at first then let our hair grow out as we moved further into the Swinging Sixties.

Clarkie's parents were wonderful people. Cliff and Yvonne were big supporters of the Bombers. They came to all our home games and Cliff sat on the board of directors. They were caring too, and they often gave me and Bobby advice. It wasn't about hockey, and mainly centered on staying out of trouble or making the right choices.

Clarkie and I lived at opposite ends of town. We took his father's car, a 1955 Chevrolet hardtop, for a spin more than once. We often returned it with an empty tank, and Cliff was none too pleased about that. We finally bought our own car together—the same model as Clarkie's dad's, except with two doors instead of four. It cost us about eighty bucks in total.

BEFORE THE 1967–68 season, the Bombers moved to the Western Canada Junior Hockey League and we made a good impression. The league would be renamed the Western Canada Hockey League the following season. Today it's known simply as the Western Hockey League.

That season, Clarkie led the league in assists (117) and finished first in overall scoring (168). I finished second (131). I set a league goal-scoring record. I had 85 goals heading into the final regular-season game, one less than the record 86 Fran Huck had scored in the 1963–64 season. Clarkie assured me I would break the record, and wouldn't you know it, I did. I scored twice in that game against the Regina Pats, Huck's old team. When the final buzzer sounded, the crowd in Flin Flon gave me a standing ovation and my teammates carried me off the ice on their shoulders. It was a great moment.

We finished at the top of the standings (47–8–5) in the eleven-team league. Coincidentally, the Weyburn Red Wings, the team that had cut me two seasons before, finished second from the bottom. But the Estevan Bruins swept us in the final, and the last game was a heartbreaker. They scored with less than a minute remaining to win the game (3–2) as well as the title—in the Whitney Forum, no less. The Bruins went on to play in the Memorial Cup. They were allowed to add three players to their roster from other teams in the league. They invited me to play for them but I turned down the invitation because they hadn't invited Clarkie too.

DESPITE THAT DISAPPOINTMENT, our fans remained loyal. They continued to pack the Forum in the following seasons and send the decibel level through the roof after every goal we scored.

People knew us wherever we went and Dembinsky's wasn't the only local business that rewarded us for our accomplishments. One season I won so many free steak dinners from a local hotel that I treated the entire team to a meal. The local Kentucky Fried Chicken franchise supplied a bucket of chicken for any player who scored a hat trick. I recall winning that prize a few times. No complaints there.

As you can imagine, some of the other kids in town resented us. We got into the occasional scrap with them at the Northern Café, or somewhere like that. Some guy would make a snide comment or hit on another guy's girlfriend and the next thing you knew, fists were flying. Despite all that, many of the kids became great friends of ours and we keep in touch to this day.

I played some pool in my downtime, and thanks to all those hours spent at the pool hall in Riverton, I was one of the better players in Flin Flon. My friends and I sometimes played for a bit of money, twenty bucks here or there. That was a lot of money back then.

On Sundays, the Bombers played in the afternoons and had the nights free. We would often go to a movie and then afterwards, depending on how the week had gone and how tired we were, we would get together at someone's house. We spent some of those evenings flirting with girls, and if it was available, drinking beer. If we over-indulged on a Sunday night, Paddy would work us extra hard in practice on Monday. Paddy had a way of knowing what we were up to.

My life in Flin Flon was great, and a lot of that was due to the Reids, who were terrific people. I went everywhere with them. Some of my fondest memories of life in Flin Flon are of barbecues at their cabin on Beaver Lake. Family members and friends would gather around a big kitchen table to feast on steak, potato salad, and coleslaw. The Reids often invited so many people, including Bombers players, to the cabin that they had to set up several picnic tables to accommodate all the guests. I loved shooting the breeze with everyone. Mary was like a mother to me in many ways. She would sit me down for a stern talk when I hung out too late or did some other stupid thing teenagers do. She wanted make sure I didn't lose my way in life. I took it for granted at the time but I later realized how much I owed the Reids. They provided me with a home and gave me the guidance I needed, particularly at that time of my life.

The Bombers' board members and everyone else in town also kept an eye on the players. When we put on the Bombers jersey we were representing Flin Flon, and that meant a lot to the people there. We played our hearts out for them but we could never repay them for all they did for us—at least that's the way I felt. My experience there played a big role in shaping my life.

THE 1968–69 SEASON was memorable for more reasons than one. I got off to a great start. I had 36 goals and 10 assists in just 21 games and was on track for another record-breaking season, until a game in Saskatoon in November. I was coming around their net at one point when a Blades player coming from the other direction clipped me. I spun around and one of his teammates smashed into my right shoulder. I managed to keep control of the puck and put it out front, but I knew something was wrong. I sat out the rest of the game.

"I didn't see him much during the hockey season even though he lived with us because he spent most of his time with his teammates. But I hung out with him in the summer. We used to go to the Northern Café after dances. Fights broke out regularly, but Reggie was never the instigator. He would try to calm things down. He was mature for his age and well adjusted."

RICKY REID

I boarded the bus with my teammates for the drive back to Flin Flon, and it felt like the longest five hours of my life. The pain was excruciating. Turned out I had a separated shoulder and a broken collarbone. I flew to Winnipeg the next day for an operation. Surgeons screwed me back together then put my arm in a sling and told me to stay off the ice for a month. But what kid listens to doctors? I was back on skates in a week or two, tooling around with the stick in my left hand. It was torture not to play. Thankfully, I was back in the lineup in time for the playoffs.

The team had managed just fine without me. With Clarkie leading the way, the Bombers had marched to the top of the standings. My shoulder was one hundred percent healed by the time we took on the Edmonton Oil Kings in the final. It was a hard-fought series but we managed to clinch it in Game 6, beating them in their own rink.

Earlier in the day, the Oil Kings' manager and coach, "Wild" Bill Hunter, predicted that I wouldn't get any points in the game because Edmonton's checking line was so good. We bet on it, and he lost. He sent someone to deliver the five bucks to me in the dressing room. Bill was a friendly guy and we had a great rapport. That continued over the years and we would always kid around when we ran into each other at hockey banquets and other events.

Four days after winning the WCHL title, we headed to Ontario to take on the St. Thomas Barons. They had won the Western Ontario championship and we were playing them for national bragging rights. We won the first game. They took the second one, and it was quite the event. Officials handed out twenty-six minor penalties, three majors, and five misconducts overall. Also, the game was delayed for ten minutes in the second period when a fan was cut during an altercation with three of our guys. It was that kind of game. When it ended, the Barons' GM said he wanted the remaining games to be played in Winnipeg because it was the only chance his team had "to come out alive." Those were his exact words.

But the series moved to Flin Flon as planned and kept up what one reporter described as our "rough-play tactics." We won the third contest then squared off in a game to remember. We were leading 4–0 midway through the second period—I had three goals and an assist—when the second brawl of the game broke out. The Barons skated off the ice and never came back. Mounties escorted them back to their hotel—better safe than sorry—and we celebrated our default win in the usual way. We wrapped our arms around each other to form a big circle and recited a chant while skipping from one skate to the other. Full confession: we had been doing that routine in the dressing room for four seasons and I still didn't know the words. I'm not sure all the other guys did either.

ANOTHER GAME STICKS out in my mind, and that has nothing to do with what happened on the ice. In the middle of an away game against Winnipeg a fight broke out in the stands. Clarkie turned to me on the ice and said, "Guess who's in the middle of it!" Sure enough, when I looked up into the stands, it was my brother Rudy. (I had taken Clarkie home with me to Riverton a few times, so he knew my family well.) Turns out, a Winnipeg fan had called me a "dirty Indian" while I was on the ice. Unfortunately for him, he was sitting right in front of my mother, Kate, and a huge contingent of my family and friends. She whacked him over the head with her purse. That is when the punches started to fly. Rudy was thrown out but my mother stayed for the rest of the game. My mother had followed my career closely, but that night was the first time she ever saw me play.

You know, that person wasn't the first to hurl racial remarks at me. Growing up in Riverton, my buddies and I sometimes called each other names when we got into tussles. But I never thought much of it. I heard the term "dirty Indian" more often when I was playing junior hockey. Paddy once took me aside and said, "If fans of the other team are calling you names, you must be doing something right." After all, I had the puck all the time and the other guys were chasing after me. From then on, I took those insults as compliments. I made the choice to turn a negative into a positive, and that approach has served me well over the years. If you view things in a positive light, and see the silver lining when times are tough, life is much easier.

At that time, there were just a handful of Aboriginal players in the league, including Ron Burwash. He was Métis but I didn't know that until years later. A couple of other Aboriginal guys, Roy Atcheynum and Blaine Rydman, played for the Estevan Bruins. Two others, Willie McLeod and Henry Boucha, played for another Junior A team, the Winnipeg Jets. Boucha turned pro and I think a couple of the other guys did, too.

JUST BEFORE MY third season with the Bombers, I met Isabel Hunter, a beautiful farm girl from Dropmore, Manitoba, who would play a big role in my life. Isabel had recently graduated from the University of Manitoba and moved to Flin Flon to work as an occupational therapist. She helped me recover from that bad shoulder injury. She was tough with me and let me know I was a lousy patient, and I admired her for that. We began to see each other a lot. She and a roommate rented a basement apartment right next door to the Reids', where I lived. I spent a lot of time at her place, sometimes after curfew. We had to be at home by 11 p.m. the night before home games. On those nights, when Paddy called to check in on me, Mary would turn on the light in the bathroom. That was my signal to sprint home. When I got there, I would pick up the phone and tell Paddy I had been there all night.

At the end of the season, Isabel and I got married in Dropmore. Clarkie was the best man at our wedding and, when our son Jamie was born two months later, Clarkie was his godfather. I couldn't be there for Jamie's birth in Winnipeg because I was working at the mine. When Isabel called me with the news, I was thrilled. All three of us lived together in Isabel's apartment. She and I were only teenagers at the time, but we managed just fine. The couple that owned the building, Jack and Queenie Williamson, lived upstairs with their family. They and their daughters babysat Jamie and that was a big help later on, when Isabel went back to work and I continued to balance hockey with my work at the mine. They were also big supporters of the Bombers and opened their home to me and my teammates. The guys loved to come over, but not to see me. In addition to having a son, the Williamsons had two beautiful daughters.

PADDY APPROACHED ME after one road game and told me someone was waiting for me. When I walked outside the dressing room, I saw a tall, beautiful Native woman. She stepped forward and said, "My name is Jessie. I'm your mother." I was speechless. Her name had rarely come up in conversation back in Riverton. I didn't know much about her and, at the moment she introduced herself, I didn't want to. The way I saw it then, she had abandoned me as a newborn and had no interest in me until I started making a name for myself in junior hockey.

“I had just moved to Flin Flon to work for the Canadian Arthritis and Rheumatism Society. I was driving through town with a couple of girls when one of them pointed at a dark-haired guy standing on the sidewalk and said, ‘That’s Reggie Leach!’ She told us he was a star with the local Junior-A hockey team. We kept driving, but when we passed him again an hour later, she convinced us to stop and offer him a ride. He climbed in the back seat and said, ‘I knew you would be back.’”

ISABEL LEACH

Unfortunately, I was cold to her and the conversation was awkward to say the least.

But she didn't give up on me. She showed up a few more times and I started to warm up to her. I once had dinner at her apartment after a road game in Edmonton, where she lived. We ended up talking a lot. She was interested in knowing about my life and my opinions on various matters. She was a private person who didn't talk much about her life, but I learned that she had moved to Edmonton a few years after I was born and worked there as a nurse, which she had enjoyed. She had other children, but I never really got to know them at the time. We became closer in the following years as I grew to understand the importance of forgiveness and of making good choices. I eventually realized that giving me up was the best thing Jessie could have done for me. She had made the right choice.

Years later, she came to Winnipeg to meet my children. We saw each other occasionally over the years and she called for me when she was in the hospital, near the end of her life. I flew to Edmonton to spend a few days with her in the hospital and by the time I got back home from that visit, she had passed. I do know that she had come to visit me in Riverton when I was a small child as I have a photo of that visit, but I was too young to remember the photo being taken. It's good to know she cared that much and kept tabs on me.

THE 1969 NHL draft drew a lot of attention in Flin Flon because it was the first one for which Clarkie, who was a year older than me, was eligible. Although doctors at the Mayo Clinic in Minnesota had declared him fit to play professional hockey, teams were still hesitant to take a chance on him. Finally, at the urging of their scout Gerry Melnyk, the Philadelphia Flyers selected Clarkie in the second round. He was the seventeenth pick overall.

When he left Flin Flon, Bombers fans wondered how I would do without Clarkie. A lot of them predicted that his departure would hurt my game, that I wouldn't be able to put the puck in the net as often without him feeding it to me. I set out to prove them wrong—and I did.

In my new role as captain, I supported and encouraged some talented players who were new to the league, guys like Gene Carr, John Morrison, and Blaine Stoughton, and they ended up making a big contribution to the team. Paddy put me on a line with Gene at center and Wayne Hawrysh, who was in his second season with the Bombers, on the left side. The three of us worked well together. I ended up leading the league in goals (65) and overall points (111). Gene and Blaine also finished in the top ten in league scoring.

After finishing at the top of the league (42–18–0) in the regular season, we swept the Brandon Wheat Kings in the first round of the playoffs. Then we took on the Winnipeg Jets in a really tough series. They had some great players, including Chris Oddleifson, who had finished one spot behind me in league scoring that year and later turned pro. The arena was packed for every game in Winnipeg and the atmosphere was electric. We squeaked by the Jets by winning the final game of the nine-game series.

We had an easier time against the Edmonton Oil Kings in the final, which was a seven-game series. We swept to victory in four games, winning the league championship—and I won at least one more bet with Bill Hunter. That post-season was one of my best with the Bombers. I scored 16 goals and 11 assists in seventeen playoff games.

A big, noisy celebration rocked our dressing room after the game. It was still underway when I sat down for a few minutes to take stock. I had arrived in Flin Flon four years earlier as a shy, awkward kid. And here I was, twenty years old with a wife and a son. I had just finished a great junior career, and I had a lot to be grateful for. I knew I would probably end up turning pro but beyond that I didn't know what the future held. Nonetheless, I was certain it would all work out. I have always had faith.

CLARKIE WAS WITH us in the dressing room that day. He had returned to Flin Flon after the NHL season; he'd had a good rookie season in the league, finishing fourth in voting for the Calder Memorial Trophy. He got reacquainted with everyone and even spent time with his godson. He took Jamie out for a few hours and delivered him back to Isabel covered in chocolate. Jamie doesn't remember that, but Isabel will never forget it. Clarkie and I also caught up. I peppered him with questions about life in the NHL. He filled me in and assured me I would have no trouble cutting it in the league.

For months leading up to the NHL draft, there was a lot of speculation about where I would end up. The consensus seemed to be that either I or Gilbert Perreault, an excellent center who skated for the Montreal Junior Canadiens of the Ontario Hockey Association (OHA), would be the first pick. In June, the heads of all fourteen NHL clubs gathered at the Queen Elizabeth Hotel in Montreal for the annual convention and amateur draft.

Gilbert was selected first overall. He went to the Buffalo Sabres, one of two teams that had just joined the league. I wasn't next. The other expansion team, the Vancouver Canucks, chose Dale Tallon, a defenseman and forward with the Toronto Marlboros of the OHA.

Then I was taken by a team that had acquired the third pick through a trade—the Boston Bruins. The organization's head scout, Garry Young, had apparently sung my praises to their general manager, Milt Schmidt. I would start my NHL career with Bobby Orr and the Big Bad Bruins—the defending Stanley Cup champions.

NHL Rookie

(1970–1974)

HEADING INTO THE NHL, I didn't have an agent, financial advisor, or lawyer to help me with the business side of things. I think that was the case with most of the players. After consulting with Paddy, I signed a two-way contract, which meant I would be paid according to whichever league, pro or semi-pro, I played in. I would earn more playing for the Bruins than I would skating for their farm team. Therefore, since I was playing for the Bruins, I was paid about $20,000 for the season—about $120,000 by today's standards. And three or four years earlier, players like Bobby Orr and Derek Sanderson had started with the Bruins at a salary of less than $10,000. I wasn't doing bad for a guy who grew up without indoor plumbing.

AT THE END of the summer, I headed to the Bruins' training camp in London, Ontario. General Manager Milt Schmidt and Bruins coach Tommy Johnson greeted me at the hotel. These guys were hockey legends, and to say I was excited to meet them would be an understatement. I went to a team meeting later that day, and what an experience that was. I found myself in a room with Bobby Orr and Phil Esposito, the biggest names in hockey, along with some other NHL stars. I could barely wrap my head around it. I don't remember at all what was said at the meeting, but I do remember wondering, how the heck was I going to be able to play with those guys?

My head was still spinning when we hit the ice, but I knew one thing for sure—I was determined to crack the lineup, a tall order given how stacked with talent the Bruins were. I went all out every second I was on the ice. That annoyed some of the veterans, who were just easing into the season and skating at half speed. I guess I made them look bad, in a way. I didn't understand it then, but I did later on when I was a veteran and the new guys were skating at top speed and laying the body on me from the second they stepped on the ice.

I played rough at times, like I had in Flin Flon, but the Bruins wouldn't have it. They told me my job was to score goals and asked me to stick to that. A few times I tried a move I had perfected as a junior: I would push the puck between a defenseman's legs and pick it up behind him. I got hit a couple of times doing that in camp and one of the trainers told me that move wouldn't work in the NHL. But you know what? It did.

On most days, we practiced in the morning and afternoon and then hit the bar for happy hour. We had a couple of drinks and shot the breeze for a while. It was a team bonding session, and the rookies were expected to foot the bill the first time. I ended up opening my wallet along with guys like Ricky MacLeish, Bobby Stewart, and Dan Bouchard. The veterans sometimes stayed out later into the night, but rookies were expected to hit the sack early.

During the training camp, I shared a room with Wayne Cashman, who had already been in the league for a few seasons. When I walked into our hotel room for the first time, he looked at me, pointed to the far wall, and said, "Hey, Rook, your bed is over there." I was responsible for his luggage during that pre-season. I had to make sure it got from our hotel to the plane and back. That was my duty as a rookie, and I was pretty good at it, too. Wayne was very supportive. I considered it an honor to be his roommate during camp; very few rookies were allowed to room with veterans.

I had butterflies in my stomach when I headed to the arena for our first exhibition game. In just a few hours, I would be lacing up for a game against the legendary Detroit Red Wings. I walked to the far end of the dressing room, where the rookies sat together, and put on my equipment. Just as I always had, I got dressed from left to right. I put on the left shin guard before the right one, the left elbow pad before the right one, and so on. I looked around the room. Every player, veterans and rookies alike, had a routine. We were all the same in a sense. For some reason, it dawned on me at that moment that I *could* play with these guys, that I belonged in the NHL.

The arena was packed and the crowd went wild when the teams stepped on the ice. London fans didn't see many NHL games, let alone games that featured the reigning Stanley Cup champions. I was excited, too. The Red Wings' bench had some of the best players in the world. Alex Delvecchio and Gary Bergman were sitting there beside Frank Mahovlich, a pure goal-scorer whom I had admired for years. I also spotted my childhood hero, Gordie Howe. I was just in awe of him. He was forty-two at that time but he was still one of the best players around.

Before the puck dropped, Bobby Orr took me aside and gave me a tip. He told me to keep my head up because Gordie was going to test me. He was right. I was skating behind the net on one play and Howe was coming from the other direction—and then it happened. "Mr. Hockey" elbowed me in the head. As a reflex, I gave him a two-hander across the arms, but it didn't faze him at all. He just said, "You're going to be okay, kid," and skated away. I think I scared him!

I didn't score any goals in that game, which we won, but I felt pretty good by the end of it. I had no problem keeping up with the NHL players; they weren't faster than me. I had no problem going into the corners with them, either, because I was a big kid who was used to playing rough. But I did spot a challenge. In a typical junior hockey game, there were only a few very good players on the ice. But in an NHL game, every player on the ice was very good and some were even better than that. To make it in the NHL, I would have to play smart.

I had some good role models, to say the least. Orr was phenomenal. He had all the skills in spades and absolutely controlled the game. He was a great team player, too. You knew, if you were in the open, he would put the puck on your stick. To this day, he is the best player I have ever seen. He was a low-key guy who didn't say much in the dressing room, but he led by example. He was a natural team leader.

Esposito played a pivotal role in the Bruins, winning the Cup. He stood in that crease and banged in a staggering number of goals. He made it look easy when it wasn't. He took a pounding from opposing players and I don't know anyone else who could have withstood that. Espo was very strong, tough as nails. He scored a ton of goals back then, and I think he would score even more today because of the recent crackdown on obstruction. One thing that sticks out in my mind about Espo is that he couldn't stand when the players' sticks crossed over each other in the dressing room. He felt so strongly about it that he made sure everyone in the room knew he didn't like it. Espo was good to me. He was always encouraging me, assuring me I would get my chance to be a starter.

I scored my first NHL goal, during the pre-season, in a 7–5 loss to the Chicago Blackhawks, but I have a more vivid memory of another goal. We played the Philadelphia Flyers the following week and I found myself squaring off against my best friend and former linemate. Clarkie opened the scoring with a power-play goal in the first period. I tied it up in the second by sending a wrist shot into the top right corner of the net, over the shoulder of a young goalie whose name you might recognize—Bernie Parent. Clarkie had warned him about my shot before the game and, after I scored, said to him, "Didn't I tell you the kid could shoot the puck?" The Flyers won, 2–1, but I remember that game fondly.

The Bruins must have liked what they saw in the exhibition games because they kept me around for the start of the regular season.

I'll never forget arriving in Boston. It was my first time in a big city and I was overwhelmed by the din of traffic and by seeing so many people and big buildings in such close quarters. Walking into Boston Garden for the first time was also a trip. I had heard about it for years and seen it on television—then, all of a sudden, I was there. My first time in the Bruins' dressing room was my first time in *any* NHL dressing room and I was pretty impressed.

It was bigger than any dressing room I had ever seen, and the way it was set up—well, that was really something. Every player had his own stall with his own equipment in it. On my stall, I noticed, my name was printed on the wood itself and not just on a piece of tape like it had been during training camp and

“When we first arrived in Boston, we visited Milt Schmidt at the Boston Garden. We were walking to his office when we saw a giant rat run past us. Reg turned to me and said, ‘Welcome to the big leagues!’”

ISABEL LEACH

in my junior days. Our numbers weren't just on our jerseys, but also on our skates, our gloves, and most other pieces of equipment. I couldn't wear my usual number 9 in Boston because Johnny Bucyk had it, so I went with number 27 in honor of Mahovlich. Also, we didn't carry our own equipment bags. We didn't even have to pack or unpack them. The trainers took care of all that.

To start every home game, we filed out of the dressing room and stepped on the ice through the same gate the Zamboni used. The Beatles' song "Ob-La-Di, Ob-La-Da" played on the sound system as we took our first laps around our side of the ice. The rink was smaller than most and the fans were so close it felt like they were hanging over you—apparently, the boxing promoter who built the Garden in the 1920s wanted patrons to be close enough to the action to see the sweat on the boxers' faces. The fans gave us a loud welcome before every game. They were so passionate that the place erupted when one of our guys scored. The noise was deafening. When the bad guys scored, they were treated to a chorus of loud boos. Boston was a university town that followed and analyzed sports carefully and passionately, and the people loved their Big Bad Bruins.

For the first week or so, I stayed in a hotel with the other rookies. It wasn't a fancy hotel, either. There were about two or three of us. We spent some downtime exploring the city but that got a little boring after a while. We weren't allowed to move our families to town at that point because we didn't have permanent spots on the roster.

The Bruins had an excellent start to the season. Eleven days in, we were sitting at the top of standings with four wins and no losses. I spent most of that span on the bench, playing just one or two shifts a game.

I was happy to be a Boston Bruin but frustrated about riding the pine, and that's what I told Tommy when he checked in on me. He assured me I was good enough to play in the NHL but said he didn't have a spot for me at that time, so he sent me to the Oklahoma City Blazers, the Bruins' Central Hockey League farm team. I was excited about getting more ice time as I was used to logging lots of time during a game. I needed to unleash my pent-up energy and keep myself in hockey shape. I was also pleased that, as a sign of their faith in me, the Bruins ripped up our existing agreement and replaced it with a one-way contract. I would make the same money in Oklahoma City as I had been earning in Boston.

SOME FAMILIAR FACES greeted me in the "Sooner State." Ricky MacLeish, Dan Bouchard, and Bobby Stewart were already there. The Blazers were an average team overall, but the roster included some of the league's top scorers, guys like Gregg Sheppard, Billy Klatt, and Ivan Boldirev. Dick Cherry, the younger brother of Don, the most bombastic commentator hockey has ever seen, was also there. He set up a lot of goals, but he played another important role, too. At thirty-three years of age—I considered that ancient back then—he was the oldest guy on the team, and he kept us young guys in line. He and his wife were almost like parents to us, and we respected them a lot.

Of course, he wasn't entirely successful. Most of us were full of youthful energy, and, like unbridled horses, we were a little wild.

Isabel and Jamie soon joined me in Oklahoma, and we moved into the same apartment complex as some of my teammates and their families. We all shared a courtyard and spent a lot of time there together. For many of us, it was our first time living outside Canada.

The weather was almost always pleasant. It didn't get that cold in the winter and it rarely snowed. Fans in Oklahoma weren't quite as knowledgeable about hockey as those in Boston, but they sure loved the game and supported the Blazers. Some of the fan club members took us under their wing because we were so young and far from home. One of the families had an indoor pool and we spent some time there. Bobby Stewart and I were once in the pool with Jamie when his flotation device flipped over. Suddenly, his head was underwater and his little legs were kicking like mad. I panicked and turned him right side up. He just spat out the water, blinked his eyes, and kept on going. I remember that incident plain as day because I was scared silly.

I was happy with the Blazers. I got a lot of ice time and was able to work on my game. You can practice all you want, but unless you play in real games, your timing will be off. Ricky MacLeish worked on his game too, and was soon traded to the Flyers. He said his goodbyes and headed to Philadelphia. The next day, he called his wife, Caroline, in a panic because he had left his skates behind. In all the excitement about returning to the NHL, he may simply have forgotten about his skates, but those kinds of things happened to Ricky a lot. You see, he was always an easygoing, happy-go-lucky kind of guy. He never sweated the details because he was confident everything would work out fine.

IN MID-JANUARY, BRUINS veteran John McKenzie suffered a separated shoulder. Milt Schmidt called me up to take his place in the lineup. Next thing you know, I was skating on a line with Fred Stanfield and Johnny Bucyk. At the end of the month, we beat the St. Louis Blues 6–0 at the Garden. It was an ordinary game for the Bruins—another dominating performance—but it was an extraordinary one for me. Midway through the second period, Bucyk put the puck on my stick as I was flying down the right side. I cut between two Blues defensemen, Barclay Plager and Ab McDonald, and then sent a twenty-foot slap shot past the glove of Blues goalie Ernie Wakely. It was my first regular-season NHL goal. Bucyk got the puck from the net and handed it to me as a keepsake. The crowd gave me a standing ovation. I didn't say much about it back then because I was so shy, but I was really thrilled.

Tommy was pleased with my performance. The Bruins decided to keep me around rather than stick to the original plan, which was to send me down to Oklahoma after McKenzie returned and, later in the season, add me to the Bruins roster for enough games to make me eligible for the playoffs.

After he returned, I played on a line with Ace Bailey and Don Marcotte. We were only on the ice for one or two shifts a game. Rick Smith also had limited ice time. We called ourselves the Black Aces because we wore special black jerseys in practice—jerseys that indicated we weren't in the regular lineup. When Bobby Orr got injured that season, he wore a black jersey too, and was an honorary member of our little club. I really liked Ace. He perished on 9/11 as a passenger in the second plane that hit the twin towers. I actually witnessed that plane hit the building as I was working at a landscaping site in New Jersey at the time, not knowing my good friend was aboard. I'll never forget that incident, but I'll always carry fond memories of Ace.

Speaking of practices, I should mention Gerry Cheevers. He was an excellent goalie—one of the best clutch goalies ever—but he was the worst practice goalie I have ever seen. He just hated practice and he spent most of the time standing to the side of net, just waving his stick at the pucks that went in. If you hit him with a shot, he would get furious and chase you around

"I used to take Jamie to the Bruins' practices. He was just a year old at the time, but he really warmed up to Phil Esposito. When Bobby Orr commented that Jamie didn't pay any attention to him, I suggested he take him into the dressing room. Jamie always wanted to go in there. He did that and Jamie absolutely loved him. A few months later, we passed a roadside billboard that had the number 4 on it. Jamie pointed at it and said, 'Bobby, Bobby!' He knew it was Orr's number."

ISABEL LEACH

the rink or even fire pucks at you. I know because it happened to me a few times. Off the ice, Cheesy was one of the nicest guys I ever met in my NHL career. He looked out for me that season and always invited me along when the veterans went out for a meal or a drink.

Spending time with Derek Sanderson... Well, that was fun on a different level. You've probably heard a lot of wild stories about him and I'm sure more than a few of them are true. Nicknamed "Turk," he was a flamboyant, larger-than-life character, so no one was surprised when he teamed up with Joe Namath and one of the football star's buddies to open the Boston location of the famous Bachelors III nightclub. It became one of the city's most popular bars, and the lineup sometimes stretched around the block. You could walk in there and see professional athletes and other celebrities. You could see a lot of beautiful women in there, too. Many of them worked at the Playboy Club, which was just a few doors down. Turk loved the ladies and the feeling was mutual.

I roomed with most of the guys at one time or another. We sometimes killed time wandering the streets of the cities we visited. Small-town life was all I had known until that season, so I was enthralled by the sights and sounds of big cities. New York blew my mind, and on my first visit, I walked around Manhattan with my mouth hanging open. At one point, Wayne Cashman turned to me and said, "Close your mouth, Rook, or a pigeon will shit in it."

Isabel and Jamie joined me in Boston and we eventually moved into a cozy little neighbourhood about forty-five minutes from downtown. The Bruins were recognized everywhere they went, even the rookies. I enjoyed talking to fans who approached me but I had a hard time understanding some of them. The Boston accent was alien to me. I got used to it after a while, thankfully, and conversations went more smoothly.

I spent the second half of that season on the bench, too. When the regular season wrapped up, I had seen limited action in just twenty-three games (the schedule included seventy-eight games overall) and had scored just 2 goals and 4 assists. I was frustrated. I felt I was good enough to be an NHL starter, and the coaches agreed with me, but there was no room for me on the roster with such a talented group. I couldn't see it at the time but I can now—if you have a winning formula, why change it?

How good were the Bruins that season? Well, we closed the season with 121 points, a dozen more than the second-place New York Rangers, and scored 399 goals overall—108 more than the Montreal Canadiens, who finished second in the category. Also, four of the NHL's top five scorers wore the spoked B on their chest. Espo finished first in point total (152) followed by Orr (139). We were confident heading into the playoffs, but we knew we would have our work cut out for us.

We met the fourth-place Habs in the first round. Montreal had won two Cups in the previous three seasons and was deep in talent. Jean Beliveau was near the end of his brilliant career but he was still one of the best skaters in the league. Yvan Cournoyer was an excellent stick-handler and was so fast he was called "The Roadrunner." Also, the Habs had acquired none other than Frank Mahovlich from the Red Wings a few months earlier.

As it turned out, it was a newbie who made the biggest impact in that series. Goalie Ken Dryden had started in the team's last six regular season games and won all of them. He was a big man who had a great glove hand. He did the unthinkable, shutting down Orr and Esposito time and again. It turned into a dramatic series with the momentum swinging back and forth—but our guys just couldn't solve Dryden. The Habs clinched it in Game 7 and, to make matters worse, they did it in the Garden. That hurt.

I was little more than a gatekeeper in that series. I barely played at all and my main role was to open and close the door on the bench. But I was lucky in a way. Some of the best players in history skated in that series and I was able to watch them from ice level. I was transfixed by Beliveau. He was a big man but such a smooth skater, he seemed like he was floating across the ice, and that was his final season. Just imagine how incredible he must have been in his prime! I didn't talk to him at all and I barely spoke to the other legendary players who crossed my path that season—even the ones on my own team. I was a shy kid and I was in awe of those guys.

THE NEXT SEASON started the same way the previous one had—with the Bruins climbing the standings and me watching from the sidelines. Sitting on the bench game after game didn't just frustrate me, it also wore on my mind. I started to question my abilities and, for the first time in my life, I started to lose my enthusiasm for the game. By the middle of February, the Bruins were first overall and I was discouraged. I let Tommy know I wasn't happy with the situation and I guess he took that into consideration.

AFTER A MORNING skate in Oakland, I got the news: Boston had traded me to the California Golden Seals along with Bobby Stewart and Rick Smith, just minutes before the deadline. In return, the Bruins were getting Seals captain Carol Vadnais, who was one of the top defensemen in the league, and a guy named Don O'Donoghue. I would be suiting up for the Seals against the Bruins later that day, so I checked out of the room I had been sharing with Donnie Marcotte and checked into a new one.

I stepped onto the ice wearing the Kelly green and gold jersey feeling pretty good; I would finally be an NHL starter. The Seals initially carved out a 6–1 lead over my old team, but then collapsed and lost 8–6. I ended the night with one assist.

Oakland had some good players at the time. I'm thinking of Gerry Pinder, Gary Croteau, Joey Johnston, Paul Shmyr, Walt McKechnie, and some others. Gilles Meloche was a first-rate goalie who posted four shutouts that season, including one against the Bruins. The Seals placed eleventh in the fourteen-team league, three spots higher than the previous season. We finished with 60 points, 15 more than the season before.

We might have continued to climb in the standings if not for the arrival of the World Hockey Association. Heading into the 1972–73 season, the new league lured away dozens of NHL players by offering them higher salaries. Seals owner Charles Finley refused to match those contract offers, and we lost Pinder and some of our other top scorers. Our team was gutted.

I turned down a WHA contract with Edmonton because the salary wasn't that much higher and because I had spent most of my life dreaming about playing in the NHL. Also, I was optimistic that Clarkie and I would be reunited as linemates one day.

Missing some of our best players, our team went into a free-fall. We finished second from the bottom of the sixteen-team league, with 48 points. Only the brand-new New York Islanders fared worse. We finished rock bottom the following season, with just 36 points. I felt sorry for Meloche. He faced a barrage of shots most games. The final scores would have been much worse, even embarrassing, if not for him. Basically, we were an easy two points for every team.

In one memorable game with the Seals, on January 6th, 1974, I made a pass that ended up on the stick of Chicago superstar Bobby Hull. I stood in front of his blistering shot, hoping it would miss me. But it did hit me, and broke my shin pad. I needed stitches to close the gash in my leg. It would be an understatement to say Hull's shot was powerful. I also got my first NHL hat trick during that 9–4 loss to Chicago, where Bobby's brother Dennis Hull also got one. I believe I had about eight hat tricks during my time in the NHL.

The Seals lacked more than talent. We were a bunch of young kids with no real leader. The coaches (we had four of them during my three seasons in Oakland) were nice guys but didn't make much of an impact. They didn't have a system; they just threw together some lines and sent us out on the ice. In one home game, the Canadiens outshot us 24 to 1 in the first period. Our coach—I can't recall which one—laid into us during the intermission, but we didn't react. Only Stan Gilbertson, the team jokester, piped up: "Hey, which one of you guys took that shot? You ruined everything for us!" We all cracked up.

I have to accept some of the blame for team's failure. In my last season there, my plus-minus record was −61. To compare, Orr led the league that season with +84. Also, I knew how to be a leader but I didn't step up. Clarkie later told a reporter for the Montreal *Gazette*, "The Seals were never going anywhere and Reggie played like he was going nowhere." I'm not sure why I dropped the ball. Maybe I had lost some of my passion for the game after my experience in Boston. But that's no excuse. If I had chosen to make more of a contribution, Oakland might have been a better team. Instead, I was probably part of the problem.

Despite our record, the Seals had some dedicated fans. About six thousand of them showed up to most of our home games.

The Hells Angels took a shine to us and, on a game day, you would often see dozens of their choppers parked outside the Oakland Coliseum Arena. We often ran into them at a local watering hole and shot the breeze. They said we could count on them if we ever had problems off the ice. It was never necessary, thankfully.

There was a lot to see and do living in Oakland and San Francisco, and I enjoyed my time there. Most of the players lived in Newark, a suburb of Oakland that was about twenty-five minutes from the arena. When we lived there, the gas crisis was going on, so we could buy gas only on even or odd days, depending on our license plates. So most of us took the train, known as the BART, to practice.

The team owner, Finley, was really good to us. When we went on the road, he made sure we flew first-class and put us up in the best hotels. Charley O, as he was known, owned the Oakland Athletics, the best team in Major League Baseball at the time, and he reserved seats for us at big games. There were a lot of them, too: the A's won three consecutive World Series while I was living in Oakland. We sat in a designated area close to the field and waved the A's pennants we had been given. Some ball players were hockey fans, so we met quite a few of them, including stars like Catfish Hunter, Reggie Jackson, Rollie Fingers, and some others. We hung out together socially, too.

It wasn't by coincidence that we wore the same colours as the Athletics—and I'm not talking about just uniforms. Finley bought us green blazers and yellow ties. Even our vinyl suitcases were green with yellow trim. He had us wearing white skates for a while and even expressed an interest in orange pucks—but some things are best forgotten.

Finley didn't know a thing about hockey. He rarely came to our games and, on one of the few occasions when he did show up, he couldn't get past the security guards because they didn't recognize him. I suspect the team was just a tax write-off for him, but I'll never know for sure. What I do know is that he eventually lost interest in the Seals and sold the team to the league in January 1974.

Around that time, Garry Young, who had just become the general manager following a stint as coach, asked me if I would like to be sent to the Flyers before the trade deadline. In his former role as the Bruins' head scout, Young had seen me play with Clarkie and persuaded the Bruins to make me a first-round draft pick. Garry and I got along really well and I felt a sense of loyalty to him so I told him I would stay for the rest of the season.

At the end of the 1973–74 season, I headed back to Manitoba with Isabel, Jamie, and our newest family member, Brandie, who was born a year earlier, in the middle of the Stanley Cup semifinals between the Flyers and the Canadiens. I spent most of that eventful evening of her birth running back and forth between the hospital, where Isabel was in labor, to the bar across the street, where Game 2 was being televised. I was sprinting between the two buildings when Brandie was born. We laugh about it today.

The Flyers lost that series but they bounced back all right. They went the distance the following season. They overcame the odds and beat the Bruins in a six-game final to win the Cup for the first time in franchise history.

I was on the links in Manitoba a week later when Garry called to tell me I had been traded. For the second time, I would be joining a reigning Stanley Cup champion. But this time, I wouldn't be warming the bench.

4

The Cup

(1974–1975)

X

ISABEL AND I headed to Philadelphia a few weeks later to look for a home. We were both pretty excited as we walked off the plane, and I felt good about my career prospects. Clarkie picked us up at the airport and we hit the highway. Looking out the car window, we saw a gray, run-down, industrial city. It was about as different from sunny California as you could get.

We stayed at Clarkie's place in New Jersey for a few days. While we were there, I met some of the other guys on the Flyers team and they all made me feel welcome. I knew some of them already from junior hockey or from my time in Boston and Oakland. Isabel knew Clarkie's wife, Sandy, from Flin Flon, and Caroline MacLeish from Oklahoma. All these connections made it really easy for us to settle in.

Near the end of the summer, Isabel and I packed up our belongings and drove from Manitoba to Philadelphia with the kids. We settled in Cherry Hill, New Jersey. It was a twenty-minute drive from the Spectrum, which was on the south end of Broad Street. Most of my new teammates, including Dave Schultz and Rick MacLeish, lived nearby. In fact, we all shopped at one particular furniture store that gave us a team discount.

As a result, the interiors of all our homes looked similar—we all had the same dining-room sets and sofas.

From the first day of training camp, it was clear to me that the Philadelphia Flyers organization was professional in every respect, from the ownership and management down to trainers and equipment managers. There was at least one person or department overseeing every task, whether that be ticket sales or public relations or travel arrangements. It was a stark contrast to Oakland, where only a few people took care of everything.

Joe Kadlec was the director of public relations and, later, the director of team services. He was a dapper guy who wore sharp suits and polished his shoes to a shine. I never saw him with a hair out of place—and I'm sure there were times when he felt like pulling all of it out. The players were a handful in those days, and he had to work his magic to get us out of some jams. Joe could definitely write his own book about that era. He's one of my best friends today and still keeps me in the loop about Flyers activities.

The owner, Ed Snider, built the franchise from scratch and attended all the games. I didn't get to know Ed very well but I always had a lot of respect for him. Ed, who is in the Hockey Hall of Fame in the "Builders" category, took a keen interest in the players, as did his wife, Myrna. She went out of her way to make the players' wives feel part of the Flyers family, and they worked together on some interesting projects. Myrna, Isabel, and many of the Flyers' wives helped to organize an annual carnival that has raised millions for local charities. It's still going, to this day.

NO ONE IN the organization was more polished than the coach, Fred Shero. A former player and amateur boxer, Freddy was not your typical hockey coach. He was a quiet, reserved man who rarely communicated with his players directly. When he did, it was often through philosophical sayings he scrawled on the dressing-room chalkboard. Many fans are familiar with the one he wrote before Game 6 of the 1974 finals: "Win today and we walk together forever."

Freddy would also leave notes on players' stalls. Each one made a point, but that point wasn't always clear. His words could be cryptic. I recall approaching him a few times with a note in my hand, asking, "What does this mean?" He'd just give us a look and leave it for us to figure out. You never knew what was going on behind those yellow-tinted glasses, which is why people called him "Freddy the Fog." He once gave me a philosophy book. I didn't understand it at the time, but I kept it anyway and may try reading it now, if I can locate it in all of my papers. When I look back, I am grateful that he took an interest in me. He did end up motivating us all.

Freddy was an innovator. He was the first NHL coach to have assistants behind the bench and the first to use video analysis. He also had an intellectual approach to the game. When he took over as coach in 1971, he introduced a system inspired by the Soviet game, which he had studied for years. In it, forwards and defensemen worked together as one cohesive five-man unit rather than as two separate units, which was standard practice at the time. Freddy believed that a team had to be excellent at breaking out of its own zone to succeed, so he developed set patterns of doing that and he made his players practice them for hours on end. He wanted his players to win battles in the corners and the front of net, which meant taking and delivering punishment in those areas.

"All the players and their families were far from home, so we became like a big, extended family. I spent time with the other wives. We organized the Flyers Wives Fight for Lives Carnival in 1977. Almost forty years later, it is an annual event that raises money for cancer research and many charities. Reg always got involved with the carnivals. He just liked helping people. I remember him coming home from practice one day and telling me he had met a man whose daughter was having back surgery for scoliosis. Reg wanted to visit her in the hospital. We went together and he spent quite a bit of time there, signing autographs. He did that kind of thing a lot."

ISABEL LEACH

Freddy demanded discipline from his players and insisted they stick to his system—and his approach worked. In his first three seasons behind the bench, the Flyers went from missing the playoffs to winning the Stanley Cup.

YOU HAD TO work hard to be accepted on Freddy's team, so I put my nose to the grindstone in training camp and got into game shape faster than usual. Freddy put me on a line with Clarkie and Billy Barber, and we soon became known as the "LCB line," a reference to our last names.

In the years since we were last teammates, Clarkie had become a better hockey player and an even stronger leader. He went flat out every time he was on the ice and it inspired his teammates to do the same. He wasn't too vocal as captain because he didn't have to be. Sitting on the bench between shifts, he would just say something like, "Time to go to work, boys," and everyone would crank it up a notch. The players responded to Clarkie because they respected him. No doubt about it, the Flyers were *his* team.

Clarkie also cared about his teammates. He did a lot of product endorsements in those days, so he was able to get us deals on everything from cars to clothing. I recall a group of us going to a clothing store once and scouring the racks for bell-bottom pants. Clarkie also made sure everyone was included when we socialized—and we did that a lot.

WE SPENT MORE than a few hours at Rexy's, a bar and restaurant in South Jersey. We would meet there for drinks after practices and home games. It became known as our hangout, and fans would show up just to see us. People would line up for hours to get in. The owner, Pat Fietto, became our friend and we would sometimes have dinner with him.

This may seem odd given how devoted current NHL players are to physical fitness, but when I was playing, drinking and smoking cigarettes were as much a part of NHL life as commercial flights and the beat reporters who traveled with us. By the way, you could even smoke on the planes back then—hard to believe these days. At one point during my time with the Flyers, the team brought in a nutritionist. She didn't tell us to stop drinking; she just told us to drink one glass of water for every beer we downed. One guy, who was known to be a little tight with his money, stood up, knowing that glasses of water were free (there was no bottled water at that time), and said, "I'll buy all the water from now on!"

I think the time we spent together off the ice contributed to our success as a team. If you have a team of guys who enjoy each other's company, you can accomplish a lot. I don't think you see that bond with as many teams today. Many players seem to approach the game like a business and view their teammates more as work associates than friends or family.

BILLY WAS IN his third season with the Flyers when I arrived. He was a solid all-round player with a good scoring touch. He was also a great guy, and we often sat beside each other on the team bus. When we passed trucks on the highway, Billy would sometimes joke about becoming a long-haul trucker if his hockey career sputtered. He once pointed at a boat stuck in a swamp—we passed it every time we headed to New York—and suggested we buy it and turn it into a restaurant. That never happened, of course, but it made for good conversation.

Bill Flett had played on Clarkie's line before I arrived. He scored 43 goals in the 1972–73 season but notched fewer than half that the following year and was traded away the same week

I joined the team. Clarkie told reporters I would have no problem matching Flett's numbers because I could score 45 goals in a bad season. The pressure was on.

WE STEAMED THROUGH the first few months. The day after Christmas, we beat the Washington Capitals 4–1 and broke a club record by going unbeaten in twelve straight games. I scored in that game—one of a handful of times I put the puck in the net early that season. I was so focused on back checking, which I was supposed to do under Freddy's system, that I lost my scoring touch. Finally, Clarkie told me to focus more on what I did best—shooting the puck. He said he and Billy would pick up the slack in our own zone. That is when I started racking up the points.

To be honest, I've never been able to understand why a team would a recruit a player because he has a certain set of skills, only to turn around and ask him to play another way. It still happens today. Freddy once asked me why I didn't pay more attention to back checking and I said, "Freddy, I'm getting paid to score goals. If you want me to play defense too, you'll have to pay me more money." He looked at me from behind those big glasses and just shook his head. We had a good laugh.

Teams had a hard time defending against the LCB line because rather than skate along the boards, Billy and I crisscrossed as we headed up the ice, and when one of us was within shooting range, Clarkie would put the puck on our stick. If it didn't work the first time, we would circle around and try again. We were in constant motion, improvising as we went. It was similar to the Soviet attack. Another key to our success was our attitude. None of us cared who scored the goals, just as long as the puck went in the net. Clarkie could have scored at least 50 goals a season if he wanted to, but he got more of a thrill setting us up. We ended up being one of the league's top-scoring lines.

IT HELPED THAT we had a lot of room to skate. The guys who played against us knew they couldn't push us around. If they did, they would have to answer to one of our enforcers, and those guys scared the heck out of everyone.

We called Don Saleski "Big Bird" because he had the same wild hair as the *Sesame Street* character—but opponents didn't find him as lovable as the puppet, not even close. He liked to mix it up and was world-class instigator. Andre Dupont, a man so big we called him "Moose," dropped the gloves too many times to count. But still, he would put the puck in the net once in a while, and when he did, he would run on the spot, lifting his knees almost to his waist. Fans loved the "Moose Shuffle."

Bob Kelly was relentless and would chase the puck like a bloodhound. He wasn't tall but he had a solid build, and when "Hound" threw his weight around, it made an impact. Freddy once said we should "take the shortest route to the puck carrier and arrive in an ill humor," and no one took those words to heart more than Hound. He would make a beeline for the puck and bowl over anyone in his way, even players from his own team. He once ran into me so hard, he knocked the wind out of me. I think he ran over every guy on our team at least once.

But no one was more intimidating than Dave Schultz. He was more than just an enforcer. He was the most feared fighter in the NHL and had led the league in penalties for two straight seasons. When things got rough on the ice, Freddy would send him out with Clarkie. No one would take a run at our captain when "The Hammer" was within striking distance—and those who did paid a heavy price. Schultzie would drop the gloves, take two or three punches to his head just to get set, then start wailing away with his fists. He would keep going until the officials stepped in. Believe it or not, I never saw him bleed. Schultzie knew what his job was and he did it well. Every guy on that team had a specific role to play and no one had a problem with that. We all bought in to the program.

Schultzie didn't start out as an enforcer, though. When I was with the Flin Flon Bombers, he skated for the Swift Current Broncos. He was known around our junior league as a goal-scorer. In one season, he notched 69 points in fifty-nine games. There were a lot of brawls in those days, but he was never involved. But when he was playing for the Salem Rebels, the Flyers' farm team in the Eastern Hockey League, Schultzie realized he wouldn't make it to the NHL on his offensive talent alone, so he did what he had to do get where he wanted to go. He started using his fists.

I found that out during my last season with the Seals. In the second period of a game against the Flyers, one of our defensemen, Barry Cummins, whacked Clarkie on the head with his stick, and that triggered a bench-clearing brawl. Schultzie was in the thick of that fracas. He also started one later in the period, squaring off against one of our forwards, a guy named Hilliard Graves. I was paired up with some guy in that first brawl, but I can't remember who. I don't recall much more about it except that I was hoping two or three guys wouldn't jump me. That happened sometimes.

Six months later, Schultzie gave New York Rangers defenseman Dale Rolfe such a severe beating in the semifinals, people were still talking about it when I joined the team.

Believe it or not, Schultzie was a quiet, easygoing guy away from the rink. He could never explain what came over him when he stepped on the ice, so we all decided he must have had a screw loose. One Christmas, Kelly bought him a toy tool kit and told him it was to fix the loose screw. Schultzie was great company then and he still is. He's one of my closest friends today and we do a lot of fundraising work together.

No doubt about it, our team played a rough brand of hockey, so rough that we led the league in penalty minutes, with 1,953. That worked out to an average of 24 minutes in the box every game. Schultzie set a league record with 472 penalty minutes. I didn't fight much with the Flyers—that wasn't my role—but I was fine with the way we played. Hockey was a rough game in those days, and the Boston Bruins and St. Louis Blues were intimidating opponents before the Flyers. We just raised it to another level. I probably would have scored more goals if we weren't playing shorthanded so often, but that didn't bother me. We were winning games.

It's worth noting that in those days, hockey equipment didn't provide the same protection as it does today. Our shoulder pads were made from a thin felt material, and our elbow and shin pads were much smaller, and made from thin plastic or leather. We also didn't wear helmets, face shields, or neck guards. We were always mindful of that, so we were careful with each other on the ice. We took pains to avoid causing head injuries—except when we dropped the gloves, of course. It's much different today. Modern equipment provides so much protection that players can be reckless, which sometimes leads to more serious injuries. And the way shoulder and elbow pads are designed today, they could almost be used as weapons themselves.

WHEN I ARRIVED, Philadelphia was a gritty, blue-collar town that had fallen on hard times. Businesses and factories were shutting down and the crime rate was going up. Sports fans were starved for a winning team—the city's professional baseball, basketball, and football teams were struggling—and we were a rough, lunch-bucket team that had just won a championship. It was a match made in heaven. Fans packed the Spectrum for home games and waited for hours to greet us outside the arena on the University of Pennsylvania campus where we practiced. They even showed up in the thousands to watch our annual charity golf tournament.

We were recognized at gas stations, malls, restaurants—everywhere we went. I signed my name on ticket stubs, napkins, and even body parts. A woman once asked a few of us to sign her bare chest. So I put "Reg" on one breast and "Leach" on the other. That would be a shocking request today but it wasn't back then; the streaking fad was at its peak in the mid-70s. When I was playing for the Seals, a woman once took off her clothes, put on her skates, and took a whirl around our rink during intermission. When the Flyers won the Cup in 1974, thousands of people ran onto the streets—some wearing nothing but the smiles on their faces.

NO ONE GOT more attention than Bernie Parent, the best goalie in the NHL. In the season before my arrival, he posted the best goals against average in the league and finished first in wins and shutouts. He also won the Vezina Trophy and the Conn Smythe Trophy. That made him a topic of conversation on radio shows and barstools across the city. I couldn't even count the number of times I spotted cars with bumper stickers that read "Only the Lord saves more than Bernie Parent." But it was more than his success that made him popular with everyone. He always seemed to have a smile on his face.

Bernie had a few quirks—for example, he liked the smell of fresh leather so much, he used to sniff our new shoes. Goalies are a little different from the rest of us. After all, who in their right mind would face shots coming at a hundred miles an hour with no face mask, as goalies had done for so many years up till the 70s? For some, their elevators don't go all the way to the top floor, but you just leave them alone and let them do their thing. You don't want to disrupt their world because you rely on them so much. When Ray Martyniuk was our goalie in Flin Flon, he would talk a lot about Martians. We just went along with it. We would walk into the dressing room and say, "How's it going, Marty? How are the Martians today?"

Bernie was carefree in many ways, but he took his job seriously. In practice, he spent hours moving side to side across the goal crease and coming out of the net to cut down angles. A few times he asked me take some shots on him and give him feedback. I would tell him if he was leaving too much of the net open and he would make some adjustments. Bernie was in a league of his own. I knew that because I studied all the goalies I faced. I would watch them during pre-game warm-ups to find their weaknesses. Bernie didn't seem to have any.

Bernie played even better in the 1974–75 season than he had the season before. In his first thirty-seven starts, he had twenty-six wins and seven shutouts. We felt that as long as he could see the puck he would stop it. Bernie would keep the team in games when times were tough, so we believed him when he walked into the dressing room smoking a cigar and said, "I'm feeling good, boys. We only need one goal to win tonight!"

WE LOST ONLY two of our last twenty games in the regular season and finished at the top of the league standings with 113 points. I recovered from my rocky start and scored 45 goals overall, more than double my total from the season before. Four years into my NHL career, I had rediscovered my passion for hockey. At some point that season, a sportswriter quoted Keith Allen, who had referred to me as the "Riverton Rifle," and the nickname stuck.

The mood was light at the time and Clarkie was up to his usual antics. He was behind a lot of practical jokes that season, including one that ended with a guy coming out of the shower to find his shoes nailed to the ceiling. Another time, someone completely sawed the heels off someone's platform shoes—yes, as fashionable men we wore platform shoes in those days. Despite the sawed-off heels, the guy wore those shoes anyway, walking with his toes pointed upwards through the airport. It was hilarious. Often, I was late picking up my luggage from the carousel and found my clothes scattered everywhere, going round and round on the conveyer belt. But I wasn't the only one. It was harmless fun. None of us dared to pull a prank on one of our trainers, though. No one wanted to end up with itching powder or hot liniment in his jock.

Clarkie and I would sometimes compete to see who could chew the most gum at one time. I swear, he once shoved ninety-nine sticks of gum in his mouth. I'm not sure how he managed that. I guess he just had a big mouth—he chewed tobacco during practices, too. I tried chewing tobacco once and I didn't mind it until I took a check in the corner and swallowed the wad. I was sick for a week. I never chewed tobacco again.

One of hockey's more notorious moments took place that season during a game against Montreal. I fired a slap shot towards the net and hit Larry Goodenough, who was working the crease. The shot struck him directly in the butt. A few minutes later, Larry hobbled off the ice and went straight to the dressing room. I guess the shot knocked the crap out of him, quite literally! He had to change his hockey pants and socks. The trainers threw everything out, refusing to clean the mess.

BY THE TIME the playoffs started, interest in the Flyers had reached a fever pitch. We were drawing wall-to-wall media coverage and we seemed to be a topic of conversation across the entire Delaware Valley. The Spectrum was jam-packed for the opener against the Toronto Maple Leafs. We overcame a two-goal deficit to win that game and went on to sweep the series. Bernie was the man of the hour; he posted two shutouts in four games.

We were on a high heading into the semifinals against the Islanders, but an incident just before Game 1 changed that. In the pre-game warm-up, Gary Dornhoefer took a shot that hit Bernie on an unprotected part of his knee. Bernie left the ice and Wayne Stephenson took his place. He had played just twelve games that season, but he came through when we needed him. He shut out the Islanders and we notched a 4–0 win.

But we knew we were in for a tough fight. Our star goalie was injured and the Islanders were an up-and-coming team with a good blend of veterans like J.P. Parise and Eddie Westfall, as well as some young guns, including Bob Nystrom, Bob Bourne, Clark Gillies, and Denis Potvin. Denis was one of the best defensemen in the NHL. He was the team's quarterback and he had a booming shot. He had been named the league's best rookie the previous season. Four of those guys still rank among the top ten scorers in Islanders history. That Isles team also had very good goalies in Billy Smith and Glenn "Chico" Resch.

We won the next game 5–4 when the puck went in off Clarkie's skate in overtime. Potvin accused Clarkie of kicking it in but he didn't convince the officials. We headed to Long Island with a two-game lead in the series.

The fans there hated us, of course. Just about every hockey fan outside Philadelphia hated us with a passion. They saw us as a gang of thugs—and they let us know how they felt. In every arena but our own, they shouted at us and even threatened us. It was so crazy before some games that officials had to put up a covered walkway from the dressing room to the ice just to protect us. The glass didn't extend all the way around the boards in every arena back then, so spectators could grab the players, and they often did. Madison Square Garden was the worst. Not only did those fans shout obscenities at us, they also hurled things at us. But you know what? The more they hated us, the tighter we became as a group and the better we played. We were proud to be known as the "Broad Street Bullies," a nickname that a sportswriter had come up with while reporting on one particularly brutal game.

Bernie was back in net for Game 3 but his knee was still sore, so we made sure he didn't have to venture too far from the goal crease. We managed to hold the Islanders to just 14 shots, and Bernie got the shutout. I scored our one and only goal—a backhander over Chico's glove hand.

Before our series, the Islanders had bounced back from a three-game deficit against the Pittsburgh Penguins, and they ended up doing the same thing against us. They beat us in the next three games, including a 5–1 decision in our own building. Everything we did seemed to go wrong in that one. By the third period, we were just looking at each other on the bench, thinking, "What the hell is going on?"

But you had to give the Islanders credit. They didn't give up, and I think that had a lot to do with leadership. Westfall, who was the team captain, and the other veterans were able settle down the younger guys and get them focused. I also think it had a lot to do with Al Arbour. He was a great coach and a very smart tactician who was a worthy opponent for Freddy.

The Spectrum was packed for Game 7 and the fans were on their feet clapping and chanting ten minutes before the puck dropped. With both teams standing on their blue lines, the lights dimmed, and then Kate Smith appeared in a spotlight. The roar from the crowd was deafening. Smith was a legendary recording artist known for her stirring rendition of "God Bless America." The Flyers almost always won when her version of the song was played on the PA system before a game, so it became the team's unofficial anthem. I still get goose bumps when I think about her singing that night. I wish everyone could experience what I did at that moment—the rush of adrenaline and the excitement of being at the center of such a big event. I was lucky to be part of that. Smith blew kisses to the crowd when she finished, and Westfall presented her with flowers, hoping to reverse the hex. Phil Esposito had done the same thing before the last game of the 1974 finals. It failed both times.

We knew it was a do-or-die situation, so we burst out of the gate and were so tenacious in our checking at both ends of the ice that the Islanders couldn't get their offense going. Chico made some great saves, including two on me, but it wasn't enough. Ricky MacLeish notched a hat trick and we won the game 4–1. That was the end of the Islanders' season.

“**Bobby** Hull had a heavier shot but goalies would have time to get set for it. Reggie had such a quick release, goalies didn't have a chance to react. Ken Dryden was petrified of his shot, but Kenny only had to face Reggie a few times a season. I had to face him every day in practice. If I was in a slump, he would stay on the ice after practice and take shots at me. He would give me some pointers and I would sometimes say, ‘Shut up, Rifle, and keep shooting!’”

BERNIE PARENT

TWO DAYS LATER, we were back at the Spectrum to start the finals against the Buffalo Sabres. Some of our fans were sure we had little to worry about. We hadn't lost any of our four games against them that season, and they had never beaten us in our building. But we knew we had our work cut out for us. We had tied the Sabres for the most points (113) in the regular season, but so had the Canadiens—and the Sabres had just beaten them in the semis.

Buffalo had some great defensemen. They were big men with such long reach, they made it hard to get into shooting position. That was especially true in Buffalo Memorial Auditorium, where the ice surface was a little smaller. The top line, the "French Connection," seemed unstoppable. Gilbert Perreault, Rick Martin, and Rene Robert had combined for 291 points in the regular season, 26 more than the LCB line. Like me, Martin was known for his shot. The main difference between us was that he shot low while I usually went top shelf. In just five seasons, Sabres management had built an excellent team, probably the best one that franchise has ever had.

We managed to keep that line in check and hold the Sabres to just one goal in each of the first two games. We headed to Buffalo with two games in hand—and then took to the ice for a very unusual contest.

At one point in Game 3, a bat swooped down from the arena rafters and flew over our heads. The Sabres' Jim Lorentz smacked it with his stick and it fell to the ice. No one wanted to touch the dead rodent, but Ricky finally picked it up with his bare hand and dumped it in the penalty box. One of our veterans, Joe Watson, kidded him about it, saying he would get rabies. Watson was known as "Thunder Mouth" because he had a booming voice and was a source of constant chatter on the blue line.

The bat incident wasn't the strangest part of the game. It was really hot and humid in Buffalo that day, and because there was no air conditioning in the Aud, it felt like a sauna. A mist descended onto the ice and made it almost impossible to see. Freddy told us to shoot the puck as soon as we crossed the red line, so I ended up taking some lame shots. It was so bad out there, I skated right past the puck several times.

The game was stopped more than a dozen times and arena workers came onto the ice waving bed sheets. But it didn't help much. We could hear people in the stands but we couldn't see them, and I doubt they could see us. Bernie couldn't see Perreault pass to Robert in overtime, and he saw Robert's shot too late to react to it. The puck got past him and the Sabres won the game 5–4, their first ever win against Bernie. I didn't think the game was a big deal at the time. But four decades later, I can look back at it and appreciate what an adventure it was, playing in the NHL's famous "fog game."

Fog was a bit of a problem in the next game too, but the Sabres were clear about what they had to do: they could not lose another game to us, especially on home ice. They played their hearts out and won 4–2.

Before we stepped on the ice for Game 5 at home, one of the guys—I can't remember which one, but he'd been with the team the previous season—said if we won this game, we would win the series. That was all the incentive we needed. From the first minute of the game, we bombarded Sabres goalie Gerry Desjardins. I scored my eighth goal of the playoffs on a power play, but it was Schultzie who made the difference, and not with his fists. He netted two goals to help us beat the Sabres 5–1. When you have a good team, everyone contributes and goals come from the players who seem least likely to score.

Two days later, I woke up thinking about how I might end the day as part of a championship team. I wanted to do all I could to make that happen, but there was a small problem. I had injured my wrist and was having trouble shooting the puck. I saw the team doctor before the game and he gave me a shot to numb the pain. It helped, but only a little. I had a breakaway in the second period but wasn't able to take a shot with my bum wrist. I tried to deke out goalie Roger Crozier and failed miserably. I was no Jean Beliveau. Back on the bench, Clarkie turned to me and asked, "What were you doing? You can't deke!" He knew I never played like that. I told him the painkiller had worn off and we both laughed about it.

It meant a lot to me just to be on the ice with Crozier. He was near the end of his career then, but I remembered him in his prime, when he had replaced Terry Sawchuk in the Detroit Red Wings net. He won the Calder Memorial Trophy and the Conn Smythe Trophy while I was still a junior. He was one of my heroes and I still consider him to be one of the best goalies in history.

That game was a tough battle, and the Sabres checkers did an excellent job of shutting down our line. They didn't give us much room at all. I couldn't shake Craig Ramsay and I didn't have more than four or five shots all game.

Bernie was incredible again. The Sabres had five power plays but couldn't put the puck past him. Billy helped kill so many penalties, he started to get tired late in the game. Freddy gave him a rest and put Kelly on our line to start the third period.

Clarkie won the opening face-off and sent the puck back to the blue line. Jimmy Watson (Joe's younger brother) passed it to me along the boards and I dumped it in. Kelly rushed in behind the net and took a big hit from the Sabres' Jerry Korab, one of those giant defensemen I mentioned, but the Hound managed to skate out front with the puck and slip a backhander past Crozier. We were finally on the scoreboard, and that much closer to the Cup.

Bill Clement sealed the deal with less than three minutes to go in the third period when he put the puck between Crozier's pads on a breakaway. That sparked a wild celebration.

I spent the final minute of the game standing on the bench next to Larry Goodenough, watching the clock wind down. When we heard the final buzzer, everything seemed to move in slow motion, and the fact that we had just won the Stanley Cup seemed like a dream—since I'd turned pro, I'd always felt confident that I would someday win the Stanley Cup, and here it was, happening. We jumped over the boards, throwing our gloves down, and crowded around Bernie to celebrate. It's hard to describe what I felt at that moment. I saw my Flyers brothers' faces, thrilled with the victory, whether or not they were with the team during the win the previous year. It was a combination of euphoria and relief. I could finally exhale. The experience was so immense that some details have since become blurred while others are etched in my mind forever. I do remember Clarkie and Bernie holding the Cup and leading us around the ice in a victory lap. These days each player does his own victory lap with the Cup, but that wasn't the custom back then. It's a shame because that would have been a real thrill.

It was complete chaos in the dressing room. Snider had invited the players' fathers to the game and they crowded in to celebrate with their sons while dozens of flashbulbs went off. Paddy Ginnell had come down from Flin Flon for the series and was in the room too—and he belonged there. If it wasn't for him, Clarkie and I might not have accomplished what we did. Paddy, along with my agent, Frank Milne, and Clarkie's dad, Cliff, were my "fathers" for this occasion. All of us raised the Cup in the packed dressing room and drank champagne out of it. The moment was surreal. The guys were cheering loudly, doling out man-hugs, patting guys on the back, laughing, and toasting each other. The fact that we were the best hockey team in the NHL at that moment was quite overwhelming. It is a memory I think back on often. Bernie had even more reason to celebrate. For the second straight season, he won the Conn Smythe Trophy and the Vezina Trophy.

A few hours later, we all flew home to Philly on a chartered plane—all of us really happy. We didn't land until the middle of the night, but thousands of our fans were at the airport to greet us. We headed to the Spectrum, where our wives and more fans were waiting for us. We partied in the lounge at the arena until the wee hours of the morning.

Isabel and I spent an hour or two at home before heading back into the city for the victory parade. We took our usual route from our home to the Spectrum, but when we pulled up to the tollbooth on the Walt Whitman Bridge we realized that in all the excitement that we hadn't brought any money with us. It was an embarrassing situation, but once the woman in the booth realized who I was, she waved us through. That's when we truly realized how famous the Flyers were in the City of Brotherly Love. The fact that we got through the toll was a big relief to Bernie, who was in the car right behind us. He was also waved through without paying.

The victory parade was a blast. About two million people gathered downtown, and they lined the streets to cheer as we went by on a flatbed truck. There were two more flatbed trucks behind us—one for our families and one for Mayor Frank Rizzo, who had declared 1975 "The Year of Flyers II."

People of all races and ethnic backgrounds were hanging out of windows and showering us with confetti. One woman ran along the street beside us wearing nothing at all. The reception was just overwhelming. I wish smartphones had been around back then. It would have been great to record all that. But on second thought, maybe not!

Two hours after the parade started, we arrived at John F. Kennedy Stadium and got a loud welcome from more than 100,000 people. Freddy and Clarkie addressed the crowd, then Bernie stepped up to the microphone and the place went wild. "Oui, oui, we did it again" he said. "We'll see you again next year!" The ceremony closed with the entire stadium singing along to a recording of Kate Smith doing "God Bless America."

There was so much excitement and chaos at the time, it was hard to take it all in. We were just living in the moment. To be honest, I now appreciate what we had accomplished more than I did then. Today, when people ask me about that season, I look back and see a bunch of young men coming together and working as a unit to pursue a common goal—winning the Stanley Cup. I realize how special it was to have a childhood dream come true through hard work.

Toast of the Town

(1975–1976)

After a few relaxing months in Manitoba, I showed up for training camp in September of 1975 feeling great. With a full season in Philadelphia under my belt, I was comfortable playing our system and I felt at home in the dressing room. I had regained my confidence along with my scoring touch, and I started to step forward as one of the team's leaders.

We all stayed in a hotel during camp and spent time together getting reacquainted. Freddy and his assistant, Mike Nykoluk, put us through our paces on the ice with some help from coaches with the Flyers farm team. The newcomers showed up in top shape but the veterans didn't. We used the scrimmages to get back into shape.

As the two-time defending champions, we were under a lot of pressure to shine that season, and we felt up to the challenge. We did have one big concern, though. Bernie had shown up at camp complaining of neck pain. When tests revealed he had a herniated disc, he went in for surgery and Wayne Stephenson took his place.

There was a lot of pressure on Wayne. He was constantly being compared to Bernie, but he fared well that season anyway. He ended up playing sixty-six games and posted the fourth-best goals against average (2.58) in the league. He was a great team player and a good practice goalie, too. You could shoot wherever you wanted on him.

WE HAD A strong start to the season and were just two points back of the league-leading Montreal Canadiens by Christmas. That week, the two best teams from the top Soviet league arrived in North America to take on some NHL clubs. Super Series '76, the first of a series of exhibition games between Soviet and NHL teams, included eight games. It was viewed as a clash of hockey titans, so it generated a lot of interest. NHL President Clarence Campbell described it as "the most important and meaningful series in international hockey."

The Soviet Wings beat the Pittsburgh Penguins, the Chicago Blackhawks, and the New York Islanders but couldn't handle the Buffalo Sabres, who beat them 12–6. Rick Martin, a member of Buffalo's "French Connection Line," took shots at his opponents, on and off the ice. He said the Soviets played like finely tuned machines but didn't have as much heart as NHL players. I'm not sure the Soviets' problem was lack of desire, though. I think it may have been lack of familiarity with North American hockey. Most of us played a rough and tumble game in that era, and it was new to them. Some Soviet players had trouble handling it.

But the stronger of the two visiting teams managed just fine. The Red Army had perfected a fast, passing game that overwhelmed most opponents. They beat the New York Rangers and the Boston Bruins, and held the league-leading Montreal Canadiens to a 3–3 draw.

When the team arrived in Philly to play us, the league held a luncheon in the Blue Line Club at the Spectrum to welcome them. The Soviets kept to one side of the room and we kept to the other. We sized them up but didn't interact with them. There was no love lost between our teams. Remember, that game took place during the Cold War. It was more than just a sports event to us; it was a clash between democracy and communism, between their way of life and ours.

The game meant a little more to at least two members of the Flyers family. Orest Kindrachuk, who could be so cranky we called him "Oscar the Grouch," had Ukrainian roots, and for years, his grandparents had told him stories about being mistreated in the Soviet Union.

The Kremlin had not been kind to the Jewish population either, and that was not lost on our owner, Ed Snider, who was Jewish. Some local Jewish groups held an anti-Soviet demonstration on game day. They marched outside the Spectrum and even hung banners in the arena. The Soviets refused to step on the ice until the banners were removed.

They were taken down a few minutes before the game while we were in the dressing room. Our coaches gave us a few tips before we headed to the ice, but they didn't need to say much. We were more prepared for this game than most. Freddy was a student of the Soviet game. He had come up with a system to shut down their offense and we had been practicing it for weeks. Instead of chasing them around the ice, we would play sound positional hockey and stand them up at our blue line. Freddy wanted us to be physical but he didn't want us to spend the entire game in the penalty box. He told us to take the body but do it cleanly. It would be an understatement to say the game meant a lot to him. He told reporters that losing to the Soviet team would be "worse than dying."

Some of us had played Soviet teams before. I had played against them twice as a junior, once when the Bombers took on a Moscow Selects team and once when I was added to the national team roster for two games against a touring Soviet team. Clarkie had played in the historic 1972 Summit Series and had become the most hated man in Moscow by breaking the ankle of superstar Valeri Kharlamov. Now, hockey fans from Los Angeles to Montreal were counting on us to defend the honor of North American hockey. Suddenly, the NHL's most hated team was its most beloved.

A few minutes before the puck dropped, the NHL president came into the dressing room for a pep talk. That didn't sit well with us because he had done nothing but rip us for two seasons. He thought the Broad Street Bullies were a disgrace and he had practically held his nose when presenting us with the Cup. After he said a few words, one of the guys piped up and said, "We know what we have to do now. Leave us alone," or something like that. We didn't need him or anyone else to motivate us. We considered ourselves the best team in hockey and we weren't about to let the Soviets take that away from us.

When the lights dimmed in the Spectrum for player introductions, the atmosphere was electric. Fans booed each Soviet player as he was introduced and remained silent during and after the playing of the Soviet national anthem. But they went wild when the sound of Kate Smith singing "God Bless America" filled the building. The cheering was so loud, you couldn't even hear the end of the recording.

It wasn't long after the puck dropped that we got away from our plan. We watched the Soviets and said, "If we bang these guys around, they won't like it and they'll quit." Bodies started flying in every direction, and not all of the hits were clean.

Eddie Van Impe, a hard-hitting defenseman who had been in the league for ten years, was sent to the box for tripping in the middle of the first period. Eleven seconds after he returned to the ice, he elbowed Kharlamov, who was streaking down the right side, and the star player fell to the ice. It seemed like someone had shot the guy with a gun. To this day, Eddie says Kharlamov ran into his elbow! The Soviets screamed for a penalty. Referee Lloyd Gilmour refused to call one, so their coach, Konstantin Loktev, called his players to the bench and refused to continue. Gilmour did end up calling a penalty—against the Soviets. He penalized them two minutes for delay of game. That infuriated them. They retreated to their dressing room and refused to come back out. We weren't that surprised. We knew from past experience that Soviet hockey officials often complained when they didn't get their way.

A spectator named Dave Leonardi, who was famous for his eye-catching signs, stood up holding a big one that read, "Tell it to the Czar!" I smile when I remember seeing him in the stands that day, sporting dark curly hair, a mustache, and a look on his face that seemed to say, "Get the heck outta here!" I always loved his signs, and some of us looked forward to seeing what kind of sign he would come up with next.

We knew the Soviets would return at some point, so we waited for them, first on the bench and then in our dressing room. Sure enough, when the NHL threatened to withhold payment for the series, the game continued.

Seventeen seconds after play resumed, I tipped a rebound into the corner of the net. That opened the floodgates. We were leading 1–0 late in the first period when Ricky MacLeish blew past two Soviet defensemen and fired a wrist shot over goalie Vladislav Tretiak's left shoulder.

In the second period, Joe Watson moved in from the blue line and tapped in a rebound. Joe was not what you would call a rushing defenseman; his goal may have set Soviet hockey back forty years. The game grew more intense as it went on, and players started yapping at each other in two different languages. The Soviets finally got on the scoreboard when Victor Kutyergin beat Stephenson with a slap shot, but then Clarkie set up Larry Goodenough for a goal in the third period and we notched a 4–1 victory.

The dressing room was packed after the game and we celebrated as though we had just won the Cup. We had proven that we were the best hockey team in the world. Clarkie was banged up. A collision with Kutyergin had left him with a gash on his forehead that needed twelve stitches to close. The Soviet player had tried to apologize for the high stick, but Clarkie had waved him off. Like I said, it was more than just a game to us. It was a war.

I wasn't that tired after the game because instead of crisscrossing the ice with Clarkie and Billy, I had just skated up and down the wing all game breaking up the Soviets' intricate passing plays. That was the job I had been given. It was one of the easiest games of the season for me.

At a press conference, Loktev complimented us for doing a lot of thinking on the ice but he also accused of us being more focused on "destroying" our opponents than on playing the puck. He said his team would never "play such animals" in the Soviet Union.

Despite the sour grapes, you had to respect that Soviet team. All their lines were excellent. Their third line would have been a second line in the NHL. They were strong men, maybe stronger than us, but they didn't play a rough game and we were the roughest team around.

Tretiak played well in the Soviet net and the score would

have been more lopsided if not for him. But of all the top players on that team, Kharlamov is the one who stood out. He was a small guy. He wasn't the fastest player and he didn't have the heaviest shot, but he was a real magician with the puck. It's too bad he never had a chance to play in the NHL. He would have taken a beating but I think he would have done well despite that.

LATER THAT MONTH, we played a game in Atlanta that ended with a bench-clearing brawl. Just another day in the life of the Broad Street Bullies. After losing that one 8–4 we went on a twenty-three-game unbeaten streak. A few times that season we were down a goal or two late in the game but came back to win. It seemed that no matter what we did, everything went well for us.

We finished with 118 points, a franchise record that still stands. The LCB line played a big part in that success. We scored 141 goals and collected 322 points.* I led the league with 61 goals* and Clarkie led the league in assists (89). He also finished second in overall scoring (119 points), while Billy finished fourth (112 points), 11 spots ahead of me (91 points).

Clarkie won his third Hart Trophy as the league MVP, and he definitely deserved it. He was a consummate leader and he played with a lot of heart (pardon the pun). He played injured 90 percent of the time and never said a word about it.

I scored in a lot of games that season, and before every one of them, I knew I would put the puck in the net. Of course, like pretty much every other player, I had a pre-game meal that I would repeat if I was playing well. For example, I seemed to play well on the road when I had soup and toast, and then for home games, I ate a clubhouse sandwich with egg in it. I drank a very thin vanilla milkshake about six hours before a game, and then took a two-hour afternoon nap. On those days, I would wake up from my nap and say to Isabel, "I'm going to get one or two tonight." Somehow, I just *knew*. When I didn't wake up with that feeling, I didn't score.

But one of my biggest games didn't involve scoring at all. I was pretty excited when I was selected to play in the 1976 NHL All-Star Game, which happened to be taking place in Philadelphia. After coming off the Cup in '75, getting selected for an All-Star Game was a great accomplishment. Being in Philadelphia was a highlight all on its own. Everything was done up first class, and it was my first time playing with the best players in the world. Some of my team was there, too, but not Clarkie—he was injured, so he was replaced by Ricky MacLeish. I was so in awe of playing with guys like Guy Lafleur that I didn't even get a point, but it was really special just being there.

We got thrown for a loop in March, when Eddie was traded to the Pittsburgh Penguins along with goalie Bobby Taylor in exchange for another goalie, Gary Inness, and some cash—as you can see, Bernie's health problems caused a lot of concern. Eddie had been with the team since the beginning and he was a mainstay in the dressing room and on the ice. You were always disappointed when one of your teammates got traded because most of the time, you were saying goodbye to a good friend. But you didn't think about it once the puck dropped. You just got to work.

A week after the trade, we played a game in Atlanta. Gary had a brand-new suit, and at some point before we left the city, someone found a pair of scissors and got to work on the outfit. I'll never forget the sight of Gary walking through the airport with a suit jacket and matching shorts. That was the beginning of a prank war that lasted the rest of the season. Gary was a bit like Dick Tracy. He was determined to find out who was behind each prank, but he never succeeded. You would *never* reveal who was behind a prank because that would make you the next target. However, I will take the credit for that one now.

OUR FIRST SERIES was against the Toronto Maple Leafs, whom we had swept aside the year before. Some fans expected us to do the same this time; the Leafs had finished seventh in the league, 35 points behind us. But we knew Toronto was an improved team, with two of the NHL's top goal-scorers, Darryl Sittler and Lanny McDonald, and a star defenseman in Borje Salming.

We headed to Toronto with a two-game lead. The Leafs won the third game 5–4, and we deserved much of the credit. They scored every one of their goals on the power play. We drew 28 penalties, which set an NHL record for most penalties in one playoff game. How ugly was the game? On one trip to the penalty box, Don Saleski got into a tussle with two policemen standing nearby. A few of the guys gathered around him and the next thing you knew sticks were swinging. The game ended with the Leafs notching their first win against us since March 1973. Their coach, Red Kelly, called the victory a miracle.

Ontario's attorney general charged Joe Watson with assaulting a police officer during one of the skirmishes and possession of a weapon dangerous to public peace: a hockey stick. Saleski was charged with possession of a dangerous weapon while Mel Bridgman was charged with assaulting Salming.

We were leading the series 3–2 when the puck dropped in Maple Leaf Gardens a week later, and we hoped to close out the series that night. But the Leafs captain was determined not to let that happen. Sittler scored 5 goals, tying an NHL record for most goals in a playoff game, and the Leafs won 8–5. Sittler was very smart with the puck and he played with some good wingers. I never understood why the team didn't go further when he was on the roster.

There were four fights in that game, including a bout between Schultzie and Leafs enforcer Dave "Tiger" Williams. Schultzie got a double-game misconduct while Williams got a one-game misconduct and a few other penalties.

The next day, the attorney general charged a Leafs fan with assault for attacking Schultzie on his way from the penalty box to the dressing room. And then Bob Kelly was charged with assault causing bodily harm because he had thrown one of his gloves into the crowd and it had hit a Gardens usherette in the face. Turns out she was the wife of an NHL linesman. In the end, none of the charges against our guys amounted to more than some fines. I don't know what happened to that Leafs fan.

Two of the guys who were in trouble with the law played important roles in Game 7 at the Spectrum. Saleski scored one goal and Bridgman netted two. I notched one and so did a few others, and we won 7–3.

THE LEAFS HAD pushed us hard and we expected nothing less from the Boston Bruins in the semifinals. But Boston was not the same team that had dominated the NHL a few years before. Phil Esposito had been traded and Bobby Orr was hobbled by another knee injury, but they had a great goal-scorer in Johnny Bucyk and a star defenseman in Brad Park. The Bruins' goalie, Gilles Gilbert, was also very good. Boston had finished third in the overall standings, only five points behind us, and was one of just two teams that had beaten us at the Spectrum that season.

Wouldn't you know it, they beat us 4–2 at home in the series opener. We were tired from the long series against Toronto, and it showed, but weren't about to roll over. We won the second game 2–1 when I scored in overtime. I was standing on the left side of the Bruins' crease when a shot by Jimmy Watson bounced off the backboards directly onto my stick. I was almost parallel to the net when I shot the puck across the goal crease. It hit the inside of the far post and went in. The hockey gods sure were smiling on me that season.

We traveled to Beantown for the next two games. We had rarely been at our best on Boston Garden ice, but we managed to win both those games, and that gave us an incredible boost. We were feeling confident when we headed home for Game 5.

THE NIGHT BEFORE the game, the entire team checked into a hotel in Valley Forge. It was common for the guys to stay in a local hotel for home games in the playoffs. We had a team meeting then got together for drinks. At some point late that night, I had an argument with an assistant coach. I was pretty steamed about it and I stormed out of the building. I headed home to Cherry Hill, which is over an hour's drive from the hotel where we were staying, and I was still there when my teammates were at the morning skate. To be frank, I was still a little peeved about the argument the night before. I guess I kind of checked out emotionally and needed to be alone.

Needless to say, I wasn't in Freddy's good books when I arrived at the rink at my usual time, two and a half hours before the game. I later found out that he planned to bench me—until our captain talked him out of it. Clarkie knew me well enough to know I meant it when I said to him, "Just put the puck on my stick and I'll put it in the net."

I felt good during the warm-up and even better after the game started. I scored one goal in the first period and never looked back. I notched three in the second and one in the third. They were all good goals, too—three backhanders and two wrist shots. It was just one of those games where everything went right for me and wrong for the goalie.

We notched a 6–3 win and sent the Bruins packing. It was an especially sweet victory for me, Ricky, and the other guys who had once been with the Bruins. Boston had let me go because they didn't think I was good enough to be in their regular lineup. I can tell you it felt good to prove them wrong even though I understood they were sticking with the formula that was working for them at the time.

By the end of the game, I had set a record by scoring in nine straight playoff games, one more than Rocket Richard in 1946 and 1952. I had tied two records—one for the most goals (5) in a playoff game and one for most goals in a single period (3).*

Reporters crowded around me in the dressing room, peppering me with questions about that magical game, but I couldn't explain it. All I had done was keep shooting at the net. I hadn't really thought about it. When you start thinking about scoring goals, the puck stops going in.

The guys joked about us drinking together the night before and about me playing well despite that. Someone kidded that I should drink more before the next big game. I rolled with the joke. We were sharing a laugh and having a good time.

The next thing I knew, I was seeing reports saying I'd been drunk when I woke up that morning, or even worse, that I was drunk during the game. I even saw stories that claimed I drank every day. None of those stories were true—in reality they were false—but people believed them. In fact, some still do. It really bothers me because it detracts from my accomplishments. I was at the top of my game in the 1975–76 season and I posted some good numbers. I'm proud of that.

The truth is, I didn't drink most days and I didn't drink *at all* on game days. After the games, we often got together, and sometimes, not often, we had a few the night before. On some occasions I had trouble finding the off switch when I was drinking, and I would continue for a few hours or more. But that only happened once every month or two. It wasn't a regular occurrence, not by a long shot.

WE SOON TURNED our attention to our next challenge, the Montreal Canadiens. The Flyers had won the Cup twice but many people considered us underdogs. The Habs had placed first overall with 127 points, 9 more than us. Their big line included three of the NHL's top scorers—Guy Lafleur, Steve Shutt, and Pete Mahovlich. Blue-liners Guy Lapointe, Serge Savard, and Larry Robinson were as tough as they were talented, and Ken Dryden was one of the best goalies in the game.

We were facing a powerhouse—a team Shero described as "one of the greatest hockey machines ever"—without two of our top players. Ricky, who had led the league in scoring in the 1975 playoffs, had been out since February with a knee injury and Bernie had played only sporadically since returning from surgery the same month. Still, we were confident. We had a lot of talent, and no team played with more heart.

The series opened in Montreal. I always loved playing at the Forum. The ice was fast and smooth. It was so well groomed, I used to feel like I was floating across the rink. Even more important to me was the history of the place. So many legendary players had skated for the Habs that it was inspiring just to walk into the building. Standing on that blue line before the start of the Stanley Cup finals was a childhood dream come true.

I got down to business as soon as the puck dropped, and I blasted a shot past Dryden less than a minute into the game. Ross Lonsberry, who was a solid two-way player, found the back of the net too, and we headed into the first intermission feeling pretty good. But the tide soon turned. The Habs ramped up their attack in the next two periods and we got sloppy late in the game. The Canadiens notched a 4–3 win in front of 18,000 devoted fans.

You know, I always thought Montreal fans were in a league of their own. Not only did they support their team, but they were also passionate about the game itself. They would applaud an opposing player who made a precision pass or a brilliant save, and they would let the Habs players know when they weren't living up to expectations. To this day, Montreal is one of the best hockey towns out there.

The Habs' checkers did a great job against the LCB line in that game and throughout the entire series. Jimmy Roberts and Bob Gainey were just relentless. Gainey was a great skater and he stuck to me like bubble gum for the entire series. He was a hard hitter, too, and he wasn't shy about throwing his weight around. They were so good in the second game that Clarkie, Billy, and I managed just one shot each. But I did score with that shot.

Gainey couldn't shut me down completely, though. I scored three more goals in that series and they were all the same as the first one—a shot from the face-off circle that blew past Dryden before he even moved. For some reason, I had his number. I knew he dreaded facing my shots so I unleashed one every chance I had. Whenever I played against Kenny, I would fire my first shot of the game at or near one of his shoulders. I liked to think it rattled him a little. As every shooter will tell you, when you get into a goalie's head, you've won half the battle. I guess this is where I should admit that I used that tactic with *every* goalie I faced.

The Canadiens had some players who could put the puck in the net, too, and Lafleur was first among them. He was an excellent skater. I used to shake my head in amazement watching him glide down the ice then suddenly turn on the jets and drive at the net. He could handle the puck well and he had a great shot. I just loved watching him play. No question, he was the best right-winger of our era.

I got to know Guy years later when we both played on an NHL alumni team. I discovered he had an excellent sense of humor. Before a game in Flin Flon, he turned to me and said, "You think you own this place? Well, just watch me." Sure enough, he went out there and scored 4 or 5 goals. At those events, Guy and the others would swap old stories from their playing days. The stories were the same no matter what team the guys played on. I guess all hockey players are cut from the same cloth.

The Habs were tough, too. Robinson and Savard were big men who could dole out punishment. I'm sure no one who watched Game 2 will forget Robinson's hit on Gary Dornhoefer. It was so hard we could feel it on the bench. I think the whole building felt that one. The hit broke the boards and the game had to be stopped so that a maintenance worker could hammer the slats back into place. You could still see the dents afterwards. I read somewhere that Dorny was spitting blood for several days. I don't remember that, but I believe it. I respected

"There were pros and cons to living in the Philadelphia area when the Flyers were the toast of the town. We had front-row seats to a lot of concerts and went backstage after most of the shows. On the other hand, we were mobbed whenever we went out as a family. A crowd once descended on us at a church carnival. Jamie and Brandie were terrified. Reg asked people to move back and promised to sign autographs if they did, but they kept pushing forward. We finally had to leave. A crowd would wait for the players outside the Spectrum too, so before we walked out the doors, I would say to the kids, 'Just stay close to me!'"

ISABEL LEACH

Robinson. He was one of the hardest hitters I ever played against. He once checked me into the boards so hard it just about killed me. He wasn't dirty or mean, but he would play that way if you forced him to.

We lost a second game in Montreal then headed home. The Habs beat us at the Spectrum, and three days later, we were back there for Game 4. With our season on the line, Flyers management made an extra effort to help us stay alive in the series. They brought in Kate Smith. The crowd exploded when she stepped onto the ice wearing a pale green dress and belted out "God Bless America." It really fired us up.

We jumped to an early lead when I blasted a shot past Dryden. We battled hard the rest of the game, but the Canadiens held their ground. They beat us 5–3 and won the Cup for the twentieth time in franchise history. There is nothing worse than watching your opponents wrap their arms around the Stanley Cup in your own building. But you had to give them credit. That Canadiens team was just amazing—the best I have ever seen.

We skated off the ice feeling tired and deflated. I was exhausted when league officials came into the dressing room and presented me with the Conn Smythe Trophy as the playoff MVP. I became the only skater from a losing team to win the award—five players from the losing team have won the award to date, and the other four are goalies. I had set two more NHL records by that point—most playoff goals (19)* and most goals for one season including the playoffs (80).* Jari Kurri equaled that first record in the 1985 playoffs. It took him eighteen games to reach that mark, two more than me. And the latter record was eventually broken by a young upstart named Gretzky.

It was a great honor to win the Conn Smythe, but I would have gladly exchanged that trophy for the one that was in the

Habs' dressing room at that moment. The Cup means more than any individual award. I'm not sure all today's players feel that way, though. I suspect some view the game as a business more than anything else—and individual awards often put money in their pockets.

Many people saw our pain as a gain for hockey. Les Glorieux had beaten the Broad Street Bullies. Finesse and speed had prevailed over brute force and strength. Good had triumphed over evil. But the truth is, the Canadiens would not have beaten us if they had played *their* game. They had to play rough to win, and they did. They beat us at *our* game.

One thing that still strikes me as funny: club owners around the league badmouthed the Broad Street Bullies for years while lining their pockets with the money we put in them. We filled every NHL arena we played in. No doubt about it, the Broad Street Bullies were good for business.

* Current record for goals in consecutive playoff games: 10 (Reggie Leach in 1976)

---

* Current record for goals in one playoff game: 5 (Newsy Lalonde in 1919; Maurice Richard in 1944; Darryl Sittler in 1976; Reggie Leach in 1976; Mario Lemieux in 1989)

---

* Current record for goals in one period of a playoff game: 4 (Tim Kerr in 1985; Mario Lemieux in 1989)

---

* Current record for goals in one playoff season: 19 (Reggie Leach in 1976, in 16 games; Jari Kurri in 1985, in 18 games)

---

* Current record for goals in one season, including the playoffs: 100 (Wayne Gretzky in 1983–84)

Oh, Canada!

(SUMMER 1976)

X

I WAS JUST SETTLING into the summer when I got the invitation to try out for the Canadian team that would compete in the Canada Cup. The huge international tournament would be played over two weeks in six Canadian cities and would include teams from Canada, the Soviet Union, Czechoslovakia, Sweden, Finland, and the United States. The competition was open to amateur and professional players and was considered the first real best-on-best international hockey tournament.

Scotty Bowman of the Montreal Canadiens was head coach. He was like Freddy in some ways; he didn't communicate with his players directly, but he was a great coach. He had a knack for knowing when to change lines, as well as when to replace a player during a game and who to replace him with. He had three assistant coaches, including Don Cherry, who was then with the Boston Bruins. He had strong opinions in those days, too, and he didn't hesitate to share them. He may have been a little hard on the guys at times, but he was a players' coach and he was popular in the dressing room.

I was one of thirty-one NHL players who reported to training camp in Montreal in early August. None of us were in top shape.

"I agree with people who say that was the best Canadian team ever assembled. Just look at all the Hall of Fame players who were on the roster. Winning that tournament was a huge release. I was exhausted by the end of it. The Flyers had played a lot of hockey in the years leading up to the Canada Cup. We had gone to the finals in three straight seasons. I think the LCB line was beat up and tired."

BILL BARBER

In those days, we got in shape *during* training camp, not before. There just wasn't as much emphasis on fitness then as there is today. I've heard that the current Bruins captain, Zdeno Chara, trains six or seven hours a day. Well, that would have made him an odd duck back in 1976.

Bowman and the others put us through our paces on the ice and had us do some dryland training as well. A photographer once snapped a shot of the team running around the track. Gerry Cheevers and I were in the foreground, so when the picture appeared in the newspaper the next day, it ran with a caption that said we were leading the pack. But the opposite was true. When the photo was taken, we had been lapped by our teammates—twice.

We all stayed at the same hotel and met for breakfast at a restaurant in the lobby. The waitresses got to know us and they tried to persuade all of us to order in French, but I wasn't exactly *bilingue*. I learned how to say "chicken" in French so I ordered *poulet* every day. The waitresses just laughed. It was all in good fun.

Walking into the dressing room was quite an experience, almost as exciting as my first time in the Boston Bruins dressing room six years earlier. There I was, lacing up my skates alongside legends like Bobby Hull and Bobby Orr and other world-class players—guys like Gilbert Perreault, Guy Lafleur, Marcel Dionne, and Rogie Vachon.

Team bosses built the squad around the NHL's best pairings and lines. For example, Toronto Maple Leafs linemates Darryl Sittler and Lanny McDonald came as a unit, as did Perreault and Rick Martin—though their linemate, Rene Robert, was one of six guys cut from the team just before the tournament started. Lafleur skated with his Habs linemates, Pete Mahovlich and Steve Shutt. Clarkie, Billy, and I skated together from the start of camp.

Most of us hung around with guys from our own teams, but we all got along. We had one common goal—to reinforce Canada's status as the world's best hockey nation. Team Canada was considered a heavy favorite. The Soviet team didn't include all that country's best players for reasons that are still unclear, but it was still considered a strong contender. The Czechoslovaks had just won the world championships and were also expected to give us a run for our money.

We faced them in an exhibition game two days before the start of the tournament. They opened the scoring less than two minutes after the puck dropped and were leading 2–1 by the six-minute mark. We bounced back to win the game 7–4 but we were impressed by the Czechoslovaks. Like most European teams, they played a fast, wide-open game, but they were tougher than the others and they weren't afraid to mix it up. They also had two excellent goaltenders, Jiri Holecek and Vladimir Dzurilla. We knew they would be tough opponents down the road.

WE OPENED THE round-robin with a game in front of 9,000 people at the Civic Centre in Ottawa. Before it started, an RCMP band played the national anthems of all six participating countries—*that* took some time—and we exchanged gifts with the Finns. We gave them muskrat hats and they gave us records. I don't know what became of my record or the Russian nesting doll I later received from a Soviet counterpart, but they would have made great keepsakes.

We gave the fans a lot to cheer about that night. Martin opened the scoring just a few minutes into the game and went on to score two more as we crushed Finland 11–2. Hull and Espo scored a pair of goals each and I was one of four guys on our team who scored once. It wasn't a good outing for Clarkie, though. He got entangled with a Finnish player and strained his Achilles tendon.

Another one of the Broad Street Bullies was hurt in the next game. Jimmy Watson took a slap shot to the face from the U.S. defenseman and suffered a fractured cheekbone. That was the end of the series for him. The Americans put up a good fight on the Forum ice, but we won 4–2.

We then headed to Toronto to face Sweden. Scotty told me not to dress for that game. It may have been that the LCB line wasn't firing on all cylinders, or that I wasn't in top form, but I think it was because McDonald was popular in Toronto and they wanted him to play in the Gardens. Whatever the reason for the decision, I had no problem with it. We had four right-wingers so I didn't expect to skate in every game.

We won the game 4–0 but that seemed almost beside the point. It was what happened in the stands that made headlines. Toronto fans had given the Leafs' Swedish defenseman, Borje Salming, a standing ovation when he was introduced before the game, and that didn't sit well with some of our guys, least of all Mahovlich. He threw his stick across the dressing room in anger after the game.

Toronto fans had also pissed off most of French Canada by booing PA announcer Claude Mouton because he addressed the crowd in French as well as English. Canadian Prime Minister Pierre Trudeau voiced concern and Rene Levesque, leader of the separatist party in Quebec, went a step further by saying the fans' actions had widened the gap between French- and English-speaking Canadians. He said relations between the two had not been as bad since before the Second World War, when they had argued over mandatory military service. Who says hockey is just a game in Canada?

Two days later, we faced the Czechoslovaks again. Dzurilla was between the pipes that night. He fell on the ice while skating to the crease to start the game, and that drew a few chuckles, but his play was no laughing matter. He was outstanding for the entire game. He robbed me on a shot from close in and he made big saves on Hull, Gainey, and Clarkie, who had returned to action in the Sweden game. Rogie Vachon was spectacular in our net and the game turned out to be a real goaltenders' duel. Czech star Milan Novy scored the only goal of the game to clinch victory for his team.

We didn't have time to dwell on that loss, though. We had to prepare to play the Soviets in our last round-robin game, and there was a lot riding on it. The winner would advance to the best-of-three finals against Czechoslovakia.

We managed to carve out a 2–1 lead by the end of the first period. The Soviets came on strong but we hung on for a 3–1 win. They blamed the loss on the biased officiating—their same old song and dance—but I think Orr was the reason we won. He was outstanding.

As I said earlier, Orr had all the skills in spades and he controlled the game whenever he was on the ice. He was recovering from knee surgery during that tournament and was in rough shape. But he played better on one good knee than the rest of us did on two. I'm convinced that if he had been in his prime in the 1980s, when the game was wide open, he would have scored 200 points a season. There is no doubt in my mind that he's the best hockey player in history.

TOP LEFT On most days, I spent time on top of this post, not in front of it. I was a pesky little guy and they perched me up there to keep me out of the way.

TOP RIGHT I was lucky to grow up as part of a warm, loving family. Pictured (left to right) are my brother Rudy, sisters Dorothy and Connie, and my mom, Kate, holding a smiling me!

BOTTOM My biological parents, Archie and Jessie, made the right choice in sending me to Riverton. This photo shows them visiting me a couple of years after I was left with my grandparents.

TOP LEFT Clarkie (front row, second from the left) and I (second row, second from the right) were inseparable during our days with the Flin Flon Bombers.

BOTTOM LEFT Yes, I ventured into our own end from time to time!

ABOVE I didn't get much ice time in Boston, but I had a front-row seat to some classic NHL games.

ABOVE I finally hit my stride when I was traded to Philadelphia.

TOP RIGHT The LCB line jelled as a unit in the Canada Cup. That makes me wonder why we were all looking in different directions in this photo.

BOTTOM RIGHT Prince Charles is one of many celebrities I have been lucky enough to meet. I'm not sure what he was laughing at when this photo was taken in Flin Flon—my sideburns or Clarkie's glasses.

ABOVE The LCB line was one of the best in the NHL in the 1970s.

RIGHT You don't often see this kind of photo on an NHL team's yearbook, but I have always been proud of my heritage.

PHILADELPHIA FLYERS YEARBOOK 1976-'77
PRO
LEAGUE
AUTHENTICS
PHILADELPHIA

ABOVE It was an honor to win the Conn Smythe Trophy in 1976, but I would have been happier to hold the Stanley Cup.

ABOVE We could never pry that stick out of Jamie's hands.

ABOVE Brandie has always been a natural athlete. Here she is showing me a thing or two about skating.

TOP RIGHT I was delighted that my grandmother got to know Isabel and my kids.

BOTTOM RIGHT Jamie learned a lot from watching me and the other Flyers on the ice. Seeing him play in his first NHL game a few years after this photo was taken filled me with pride!

LEFT Jamie and Brandie have always been close. A man couldn't ask for better kids.

RIGHT I attend powwows with Dawn to strengthen my involvement in Aboriginal traditions.

ABOVE Dawn and I love spending time with the grandchildren, Hunter, Jaden, and Jaxon.

ABOVE It was great to meet a new generation of stars in 2008. Hockey players of all ages are cut from the same cloth.

TOP RIGHT The people of Riverton have been staunch supporters of mine from day one, and I'm proud to say I grew up there.

BOTTOM RIGHT I encourage young people to make the right choices in life.

Riverton...
proud home of the
Riverton Rifle
Reggie Leach
Goals .... You Need Them to Achieve.

ABOVE I put the Flyers jersey on again to play in the 2012 Winter Classic. I lost a step or two (or three), but it was a thrill nonetheless.

"You had Barber on the left side. He had a great shot and was a pretty good skater. Leach had that incredible shot on the right side—and you had that super pest in the middle. Clarke played with a grittiness, almost a dirtiness. That line had great chemistry. As an opponent, Leach wouldn't always beat you in the corners, out-muscle you or out-skate you, but he didn't need a lot of chances to put the puck in the net. He had a great release."

LARRY ROBINSON

WE STAYED IN Toronto to prepare for the best-of-three finals against Czechoslovakia, and the atmosphere there was so charged it felt like a playoff game. Luckily for us, Dzurilla wasn't as strong this time out. Perreault scored one minute into the game and the Slovak goalie never recovered. He allowed four goals in the first period and was replaced by Holecek. Their team was better in the second half of the game, but not good enough. We added two more goals and notched a 6–0 win. It was Vachon's second shutout of the tournament.

Two days later, we skated onto the ice for the second game and the atmosphere was unlike anything I had experienced before. It felt like everyone in the country had their eyes trained on us, and television ratings suggested that was true. I heard that game was the most-watched television event in Canadian history at the time. Trudeau was there with his wife, Margaret, and British Prime Minister James Callaghan.

Everyone in the building seemed to breath a collective sigh of relief when Perreault and Esposito scored on the first two shots of the game. We half-expected the Czechoslovaks to react the same way they had when we jumped to an early lead in the previous game, but that didn't happen. They replaced Holecek with Dzurilla, who turned out to be as strong as he had been in the round-robin.

The game was tied 2–2 from the second minute of the third period until Clarkie scored on a power play with about 12 minutes remaining. Hull and Perreault got the assists—Scotty was mixing and matching lines at that point. That was the only goal and one of just 3 points Clarkie notched in that series.

I didn't rack up the points in that tournament either. I had some good shots but had trouble finding the back of the net. I tallied 1 goal and 1 assist over six games. Some of the others had the same problem, but I don't know why. Maybe we could have used a few more tune-ups to get our timing right. Overall, I think my performance was just above average.

The Czechoslovaks pulled even and went ahead within a single minute late in the third period. Then, with about two minutes remaining, Clarkie carried the puck up the ice and, when he crossed the line, he dumped it in to the right of the Dzurilla. I made a beeline to the corner. I saw Billy charging in with no one covering him so, as soon as I had the puck on my stick, I threw it front of the net. Billy blasted a one-timer past Dzurilla and that set off a frenzied celebration.

When we headed into the dressing room at the end of regulation time, there was no doubt in my mind that we would win it. As a professional athlete, you *never* think you're going to lose. The overtime was about as dramatic as they come, with the Czechoslovaks fighting to stay alive and us desperately trying to wrap it up. Two of our goals were disallowed. Lafleur's goal was called back because the net was off its moorings, and Lapointe's marker was disallowed because it went in the net at the exact same second the siren sounded to end the first ten minutes of the overtime period.

Finally, just after the start of the second half of the overtime period, Sittler rushed up the left side of the ice. He faked a slap shot and fooled Dzurilla. When the goalie moved forward, the Leafs captain swung wide and shot the puck into the open side of the net. The arena exploded. It sounded like a bomb had just gone off. I jumped over the bench and crowded around Sittler with all the others. It felt as great as winning the Cup, maybe even a little better. I felt like the luckiest person in the world that night. Playing in a tournament with and against the best hockey players in the world was one of the biggest thrills of my life.

When we gathered at center ice to shake hands with our opponents, Mahovlich and one of the Czechoslovak players exchanged jerseys, a tradition in international hockey, and we all followed suit. I exchanged jerseys with a right-winger named Frantisek Cernik. I tracked him down on Facebook recently, introduced myself, and asked him if he wanted to switch back, but he never answered me. Hey, it's great to have someone else's jersey from the biggest tournament of your life, but how much better would it be to have your own?

By the time Trudeau presented us with the Canada Cup, most of us were wearing our Czechoslovak jerseys. Anyone looking at photos of the trophy presentation today might think he was awarding the prize to the Czechs instead of the Canadian team if they didn't recognize us. Thankfully, when the prime minister congratulated Clarkie, our captain wasn't wearing *any* jersey—just his equipment and that gap-toothed grin.

Dzurilla and Sittler were named the best players on their respective teams—it capped off an amazing year for the Leafs captain—and Orr was named the tournament's most valuable player. No one was more deserving, at least not in my opinion.

The dressing room was hot, humid, and jam-packed. Someone had written in big letters on the chalkboard, "WIN." Most of the reporters were clustered around Sittler and Vachon; Vachon had made some key saves late in the game and was named our team's top player of the series. Sittler described our squad as the greatest Canadian team ever assembled and, looking back at the many Hall of Fame players on that roster, I have to agree.

ALMOST THIRTY-TWO YEARS later, we were special guests at one of the games of the 2008 world hockey championship in Halifax, Nova Scotia. To honor us, the Canadian players wore vintage 1970s-era jerseys for their showdown with the Americans, and during the first intermission, organizers played a video montage of the 1976 Canada Cup. The crowd gave us a standing ovation.

It was great to meet some of the game's rising stars in person at that event, including Jonathan Toews, Rick Nash, and Ryan Getzlaf, but it was even better to reconnect with my old teammates and share our memories of the historic series. Scotty Bowman, who spoke on our behalf at a special reception, could recall the competition from memory, and in detail—by that I mean how the plays unfolded in each of the games. That certainly brought back a lot of memories. Scotty also mentioned how he'd had a son that year and named him Bobby after the three famous "Bobbies" on that championship team. If I recall correctly, his son joined him at the reunion to meet his namesakes.

At one point during our visit, the guys agreed that it would be nice if we had commemorative rings from the 1976 Canada Cup. Who knows—it may happen one day. But even if it doesn't, there is no chance any one of us will ever forget that tournament.

7

Broad Street Departure

(1976–1982)

THEY SAY CHANGE is the only constant in life, and that is certainly true in professional hockey. No roster stays the same for long, no matter how successful the team—and that went for the Broad Street Bullies, too.

Just before the 1976–77 season, Dave Schultz was traded to the Los Angeles Kings in exchange for two draft picks. The Hammer was popular with our fans—many considered his swollen, stitched-up mug the face of the Bullies—and they weren't happy to see him go. They gave him a standing ovation when he returned to the Spectrum with his new team, but the love didn't last long. He cross-checked Ricky MacLeish and picked a fight with our new tough guy, Paul Holmgren. Homer came out on top in that scrap and Schultzie was given a game misconduct. The fans booed him as he left the ice. So much for a warm welcome.

Barry Ashbee had been a Flyers defenseman for four years until an eye injury ended his career in the 1974 playoffs. He then became an assistant coach and played an important role in making our defense corps one of the best in the league. Barry was diagnosed with leukemia in April 1977 and died a month later. It was a complete shock. How could a disease take down such a strong person so quickly? We couldn't really wrap our heads around it. We attended his funeral in Toronto while about a thousand people attended a memorial service for him at the Spectrum. His loss was a big blow.

In June 1978, Gary Dornhoefer retired after fourteen years in the NHL. Management sent Orest Kindrachuk and Ross Lonsberry to the Pittsburgh Penguins along with veteran defenseman Tom Bladon, for a first-round draft pick. They also sold Joe Watson to the Colorado Rockies for a couple of broken hockey sticks. His career ended soon after when he shattered his leg in an on-ice collision.

In the two seasons following our dramatic showdown with the Habs, we finished second and fourth in the standings respectively, but we were eliminated by the Bruins in the semifinals both years.

Freddy was unhappy with the way things were going and he handed in his resignation. The Flyers rejected it and said they expected him to honor the remaining year on his contract. Freddy took his case to the press, telling reporters he felt it was time to move on. He even suggested that his coaching days were over. But they weren't. Management made a deal with the New York Rangers, and Shero ended up behind their bench. Bob McCammon, who had been coaching the Flyers' AHL affiliate, took his place. Freddy was a great man and, in my opinion, his departure marked the end of the Broad Street Bullies.

IN THE FIRST few seasons after our run to the 1976 finals, my numbers dropped like a stone. I scored 24 goals in the 1977–78 campaign, less than half the total from my best season. Freddy benched me for a few games and stepped up his demands for me to do more back checking. I didn't drink much in those years, often going without a drink for months, but the slump continued. At one point Dorny quipped, "You're not putting the puck in the net and you're grumpy. Maybe you should go back to drinking!"

I tried to break out of the slump. I even stayed on the ice after practice when Freddy asked me to do some extra skating. I knew full well that I could be traded at any time. But the slump continued.

Clarkie and Billy didn't struggle like me in those years, but their point totals dropped too. Bernie showed flashes of brilliance but he wasn't playing as well as in the past. His performance improved after his childhood hero, Jacques Plante, became our goalie coach, but his comeback ended during a game in February 1979, when Jimmy Watson accidentally poked his stick blade through the right eyehole of Bernie's mask. The injury destroyed his depth perception and ended his career. Bernie had always been a big presence on the ice and in the dressing room, so it was a big loss for us.

We finished fourth overall in the standings in the 1978–79 season. We beat the Vancouver Canucks in a preliminary round and advanced to the quarter-finals against the New York Rangers and their new coach, Freddy Shero. We notched a 3–2 overtime win in the first game but we lost the next four—and none of them were close. We were out-scored 28–8 in that series. It was a huge embarrassment.

HEADING INTO THE 1979–80 season, our team didn't look much like the one that had clinched two straight Cups. We may have been a little worn out from all our past hijinks and living the high life in Philly. And our lineup had changed, too. With the exception of the LCB line and a handful of others, including Ricky, Jimmy, Bob Kelly, and Moose Dupont, the players on our roster were relatively new additions. Some of them were experienced players whose careers had been steady but average—guys like Norm Barnes, Frank Bathe, and Mike Busniuk—and others were newbies. Kenny Linseman and Behn Wilson had only three pro seasons between them, and Brian Propp was a rookie. He would go on to have an outstanding NHL career, but at that time, he was still wet behind the ears.

He and I played on the same line now and then. We would skate up our respective wings then cut toward the center to avoid going offside. It took us a while to get that right. We collided in the middle of the ice more than once and got ribbed about it back on the bench. "Nice one," someone would pipe up. "Best hit of the game!"

No one expected much of our team that season, but it turned out to be one of the best in franchise history. After we got waxed by the Atlanta Flames 9–2 in our second game of the season, Clarkie called a meeting and we all agreed enough was enough. We pulled up our socks and didn't lose again for almost three months. Our thirty-five-game unbeaten streak set a league record that still stands.

Just like in '76, in '80 I was called up to play in the NHL All-Star Game, along with several other Flyers. It was an event for the books and a passing of the torch, as it was the first All-Star Game for Wayne Gretzky and the final one for fifty-three-year-old Gordie Howe. It was also the one and only time I played with the "Great One" as a teammate. At the end of the game, which we lost, I was recognized as MVP, notching a goal and an assist—but many in the crowd felt that Gordie should have been given the honor. I do wish myself that he had received some formal recognition that night.

People wondered how our team could have been so successful that season. The answer, in my opinion, was our coach. Pat Quinn had replaced McCammon behind the bench midway through the previous season. Quinner was a big man who had a big presence. When he walked into a room chomping on a cigar, people would turn and look at him. He was a decent guy who was nice to people. He was tough but fair. Most importantly, Quinner was a players' coach. We knew he would go to the wall for us and we played our hearts out for him.

Of course, I should mention that I knew him before he became our coach. I skated against him when he was a defenseman in the league. He was a tough customer during his nine-year NHL career. You had to keep your head up when he was on the ice because he could squash you like a bug along the boards. He knocked Bobby Orr unconscious in the 1969 playoffs. To this day, there is a debate about whether he threw Orr a shoulder or an elbow. Maybe it was a little bit of each.

No one was happier about Quinner's arrival than me. He seemed to sense that I had checked out mentally and he made an effort to bring me back into the fold. He took me aside in training camp and told me he wanted me to kill penalties. I'm sure a few people laughed at that. I hadn't made my name as a two-way player, after all. But I worked hard on that part of my game all season and enjoyed my new role. The more ice time I got, the more fun I had and the better I played. I finished the season with 50 goals and 76 points. Quinner deserved most of the credit. I could be a hard guy to motivate, but he found a way.

As a former player, Quinner knew that the better the guys got along off the ice, the better the team would do on the ice. He encouraged us to socialize with each other away from the rink. When we arrived in a city the day before a game, we would go to practice then meet for dinner, hang out, and swap stories. We became a band of brothers.

My house became an informal meeting place for my teammates. Isabel and I told the guys they could come over anytime, whether or not we were home, and a few of them took us up on the offer. One night, we were all asleep when Brandie heard some noise in the backyard and looked out her bedroom window to see people splashing around in the pool. Many of my teammates and other members of the Flyers organization spent time there, even when Isabel, the kids, and I were at home in Manitoba for the summer. Joe Kadlec and his family were kind enough to look after the pool during those months.

Propper lived with us when he first arrived in Philadelphia—a lot of the young guys did. The Clarke family also lived with us for a while when their house was undergoing renovations. Larry Goodenough and his family lived with us too, until they found their own place.

WE LOVED LIVING in Cherry Hill. We made some great friends in the neighborhood and would get together with them for dinners and other events. Until then, I hadn't spent much time with people outside of the hockey world, so those friendships broadened my horizons. We all got together for meals or to play cards. We became very close to two families in particular, the Acchiones and the DiCiccos. They made us feel like family at their dinners, which were typically old-style Italian food. Isabel and I keep in touch with some of these people to this day. Their kids are still friends with Jamie and Brandie.

Tastykake, a Philadelphia-based company that produces baked goods, would give me a case of treats for every goal I scored. I would donate some of them to the children's hospital and to local charities. Most of the other cases ended up at home and in the hands of Jamie, Brandie, their friends, and our neighbors. Just imagine how many Tastykakes were consumed in Cherry Hill during the 1975–76 season, when I scored 80 goals!

I would always leave some autographed photos at the house for Isabel to hand out when I wasn't there. At one point, she discovered our kids were actually selling the photos to other kids for a dollar apiece. She put an end to their business venture and ordered them to return the money. I think their overall sales had amounted to twenty-five dollars. Maybe that is how my kids first learned their business skills!

WE FINISHED AT the top of the standings that season, with 116 points. We met the Edmonton Oilers, one of four franchises that had joined the league that season, in the best-of-five preliminary round. The Oilers fought hard and pushed the third game into double overtime, but we won 3–2 and sent them packing. Gretzky was just a teenager then, but he was already one of the best players in the league. He always seemed to know how plays would unfold. You could see he was destined for great things.

We faced the Rangers in the quarter-finals for the second straight season, but the results were flipped this time. We beat them four games to one. The outcome was the same in our semifinals against the Minnesota North Stars. They had some firepower in Al MacAdam and a few others, but they were no match for Billy. He caught fire in that series, notching 9 goals and 3 assists.

Five days later, we skated onto the ice at the Spectrum to start the Stanley Cup finals against the New York Islanders. Two young players, Bryan Trottier and Mike Bossy, were

“Reg always took such a responsibility for all the young players, the rookies who came to the Flyers—some for short stints, some the stars of the future. He made certain they had places to live, vehicles to drive, right down to appliances for an apartment. Many stayed with us in the beginning when they were getting settled in. We heard later how important that had been to their adapting to the big leagues.”

ISABEL LEACH

among the NHL's leading scorers. Denis Potvin was still one of the best defensemen around, and Billy Smith and Glenn Resch were both strong in net. We had our work cut out for us.

The Isles beat us 4–3 in overtime at the Spectrum. I felt partly to blame for the outcome. Early in the game, I didn't get down fast enough to block a shot by Potvin and the puck ended up in our net.

They were leading the series eleven days later when we took to the ice for Game 6 in Long Island. It turned out to be a dramatic contest. I scored an early goal, one of 9 I netted that post-season, then the game took a turn for the worse.

Pete Peeters, who had split goaltending duties with Phil Myre all season, made a save a few minutes after my goal but the rebound popped into the air and Potvin smacked it into the net. Some people thought his stick was above his shoulder when he made contact with the puck so the goal shouldn't have been allowed, but I wasn't sure about that.

We were still reeling when the Islanders' Clark Gillies started a passing play that ended with the puck in our net. That goal shouldn't have counted because his pass was offside, but the linesman, Leon Stickle, missed the call and the Islanders went ahead 2–1. We managed to push the game into overtime, and in our second-to-last shift of the game, I hit the crossbar with a shot. But the Islanders ended up beating us, 5–4, winning the Stanley Cup for the first time ever.

Ed Snider gave reporters an earful in the corridor outside our dressing room. He called the officiating a disgrace and even said referee-in-chief Scotty Morrison should be shot—words that might land him in jail today. I understood where he was coming from. When the calls are that bad in a big game, it gives the league a black eye. Still, officials are only human and they have bad games too. That's just the way hockey is; you never know what's going to happen. That's why I think the NHL made a good move by introducing video review. It makes the game more fair.

Quinn won the Jack Adams Award as coach of the year, and he deserved it. I'm still disappointed that we weren't able to win the Cup for him.

I WAS PLAYING under a multi-year contract at the time. It stipulated that if I scored at least 50 goals in a season, management would rip up the existing contract and sign me to a better one.

Even though I hit that mark in the 1979–80 season, I went the entire 1980–81 season without a new contract. I'm still not quite sure why. But I posted good numbers (34 goals and 70 points) anyway, and was optimistic about my future in Philadelphia when I showed up for training camp in the fall of 1981.

I was in the option year of my contract and hoped to negotiate an extension, but management refused. I was fed up by then, so I walked out of training camp. They called me back a few days later and we agreed to a one-year deal. It stipulated that if I notched 30 goals or 50 points in the 1981–82 season, the team would extend my contract for another two years. I was confident I could reach that mark.

As it turned out, I spent some time on the bench that season while the younger players got more ice time. I could see the writing on the wall, and in late February, I asked Keith Allen to trade me before the deadline. I didn't want to spend the rest of the season riding the pine. He assured me I would get more ice time if I stayed, so I did.

The team struggled that season, too, and by mid-March we had won just thirty-four of seventy-two games. I'm not sure

“My best friend, Jody Clarke, and I once went into the Flyers dressing room, erased some writing on one side of a two-sided chalkboard, and scrawled our names on it. Later, when Fred Shero turned the board around to show his players something he had written, he saw the words ‘Brandie’ and ‘Jody’ there instead. Oops! I used to go to the rink with my father a lot. During practice, I would hang out with Cecilia Baker, who ran the ticket office. She would sit me down at a desk and let me bang away on a typewriter. I had a great time. I also enjoyed driving to the rink with my father. I remember being in the back seat when he and Bob Clarke raced there in their matching Jeeps. What a ride!”

BRANDIE LEACH

what the problem was. Maybe it was a combination of age catching up to the veterans and the new kids still finding their footing. As any athlete will tell you, it's often hard to pinpoint the reason for a mediocre season.

It turned out to be the team's second straight disappointing campaign—the Calgary Flames had eliminated us in the quarter-finals the previous year—and management decided it was time for a change. With eight games remaining in the schedule, they fired Quinner and hired the man he had replaced three years before.

I was surprised. I thought it was foolish to bring in a coach who had already proven he couldn't do the job. Even more baffling to me was the decision to make him assistant general manager and strip Clarkie of his role as assistant coach, a position he had held since 1979. I'm convinced that getting rid of Quinn was one of the biggest mistakes the Flyers ever made.

I had 26 goals and 47 points when McCammon took over again, and I was sure I would get the numbers I needed for a contract extension; we were heading into back-to-back games against one of the weakest teams in the league, the Hartford Whalers. But McCammon benched me for both games without an explanation, despite Allen's promise. At that point, I was convinced that management was planning to cut me loose.

I was discouraged to say the least. I took my time getting to practice a few days later, and when I showed up, McCammon called me into his office and told me I was done as a Flyer. The team was releasing me. I was upset and I used some choice words to let him know what I thought.

I think they let me go mostly because of my inconsistent play and my age, although my total points were still decent. I was almost thirty-two years old, the oldest guy on the team aside from Clarkie, and the Flyers had some good young talent. My binge drinking didn't help matters. But I think there was a more important factor—my relationship with McCammon.

I get along with most people I meet, but I never got along with him. It was unfortunate, but that kind of thing happens sometimes. He and I mixed like oil and water from day one. Professional hockey is like any other workplace in some ways. There are personality conflicts in a dressing room just as there are in an office. And in both places, you're in trouble if you don't get along with your boss.

The club continued to pay me but I didn't play another game that season. The Flyers finished eighth overall and were beaten by the Rangers in the first round of the playoffs. On the night of Game 4, I went to the wedding of a friend's daughter. Some of the guys showed up there after the game and we talked about the way the season had ended. They said they were disappointed that I had been let go and I told them I was even more disappointed, both for them and for Flyers fans, about the way the season had ended.

I made some big mistakes in my last few years with the Flyers. I thought I was working hard at the time, but in retrospect, I see that I may not have been making as much of an effort as I should have. I didn't handle the McCammon situation properly. You should do your best to get along with people even if you don't like them, but I didn't make an effort with McCammon and it cost me. I made some dumb choices in those years, but that is what life is all about: you screw up, you make sure you learn from your mistakes, and you move on.

Late that summer, my agent, Frank Milne, called me with some good news. After eight eventful years in Philadelphia, I would be saying goodbye to my friends in Philadelphia and moving northwest to the Motor City.

"**Bob** McCammon came in with a new way of doing things. He connected well with the young guys on the team but not as much with the veterans. We had our own way of doing things. We had a bit of a beef with McCammon, but he was the coach, so we had to fall in line. I never saw a confrontation between him and Reggie but I knew they didn't get along. I could tell Reggie wasn't happy."

BILL BARBER

The Fall

(1982–1985)

X

THE DETROIT RED Wings had a horrible 1981–82 season. They finished second-last in the standings with just 54 points and missed the playoffs for the fourth straight year. When Mike Ilitch bought the franchise in June 1982, he did some house cleaning. He brought in a new general manager, Jimmy Devellano. He also hired a new coach: Nick Polano, who had spent a season as Scotty Bowman's assistant coach in Buffalo.

Devellano revamped the roster. He bought out the contracts of Peter Mahovlich and Vaclav Nedomansky and used the freed-up money to sign a handful of veterans, including me, defenseman Colin Campbell, goalie Jimmy Rutherford, and forward Stan Weir, who had been my teammate in Oakland.

The club hoped that our arrival would boost ticket sales—there were about 4,000 season ticket holders at the time—and inject the team with some leadership. Devellano hoped we would finish with at least 10 more points than in the previous season.

Polano was a nice guy away from the rink, but he wasn't much of a players' coach and some of us felt he was more concerned about his standing with the front office than he was with our well-being. He was the opposite of Pat Quinn in that regard.

Polano's approach to coaching was, "It's my way or the highway." I should have just rolled with it because you can't change people in that situation, but I didn't understand that at the time. I butted heads with him more than once.

Polano once tore into one of our defensemen so badly during a home game that the guy shoved him and stormed into the dressing room, where he threw his stick in frustration. Unfortunately, it hit the doohickey that set off the sprinkler system and the dressing room was flooded by the end of the period. Overall, I think Nick would have gotten more out of his players if he had treated them better.

Despite the friction, we held our own for most of the season. Our team had a mix of solid veterans and good young players like John Ogrodnick and Murray Craven, who would later help lead the Flyers to two Stanley Cup finals. Still, we went into a tailspin late in the season and ended up with 57 points, just 3 more than the season before, and missed the playoffs.

Some of the veterans, me included, didn't play in the last few games. I suspect, at that point, management had given up on the season and wanted the team to finish as low as possible in the standings to ensure a top pick in the 1983 draft. If the veterans had played in those last few games, we might have thrown a wrench into the works by notching a few wins. As it turned out, Detroit selected budding superstar Steve Yzerman in the draft—and we all know how that worked out for the team.

I had some good games and did some penalty killing that season, but overall my play was unspectacular. I finished tenth in team scoring with 15 goals and 32 points. The Red Wings released me in mid-June along with three other veterans—defenseman Jim Schoenfeld, forward Tom Rowe, and Gilles Gilbert, the goalie who had been in the Bruins' net for the playoff game in which I had notched five goals. Gilles had a great sense of humor and was a lot of fun to be around. He was also a real team player.

BY THEN, I had come to realize I would likely never play in the NHL again, and that was hard to handle. To make matters worse, my home life was a shambles. My spiral downwards had begun. Years of binge drinking had taken a toll on my marriage and it was hanging on by a thread. By that time, I would go on a bender every week or two—run out for a loaf of bread on a Friday and return on Sunday. Isabel and I didn't argue much in those days—I think because she had just given up.

With the season over, I headed to Manitoba. Isabel and the kids joined me there after the school year ended, and we spent the summer together.

WITHOUT ANY OTHER options, I jumped at the chance to play on a minor professional team owned by the Ermineskin First Nation and a businessman named Larry Gordon, whom I had known since my days in Boston. I signed a one-year contract with the Montana Magic of the Central Hockey League and I also had a separate, supplemental agreement with Ermineskin, which was sealed with a handshake. I headed to Billings late that summer while Isabel and the kids moved back to the Philadelphia area.

I stayed in a hotel for my first month in Billings and ate most of my meals in the restaurant. The head coach, Bryon Baltimore, who was also staying there, sometimes joined me. When Stan Weir arrived without his family, we moved in together. Stan had a dry sense of humor and I enjoyed shooting the breeze with him while watching television or playing pool. He

“Some people assume Reg drank every day when we were together, but that’s not true. He would go for weeks, or even months, without a drink. But then he would go out for drinks with the guys and get carried away. That is when things were bad. The rest of the time he was a great husband and father. The other wives would often comment on how good he was with the kids. His drinking got worse later on, when he was on his own in Montana.”

ISABEL LEACH

became a good friend. Billings was a cow town and a college town, so it wasn't hard for us to find a watering hole.

My new team, which had been based in Wichita the previous three seasons, included a mix of players—some at the beginning of their careers and others at the end. I was thirty-three years old when the season started, the oldest player on the roster. The second-youngest, Perry Ganchar, was almost fourteen years my junior. He was a speedy little guy who played part of the season wearing a pair of skates I lent him after he busted his own pair and couldn't afford to replace them.

The Magic had two of the league's top scorers on the roster—John Markell and Alain Lemieux (Mario's brother). John was a very skilled player who ended up playing in fifty-five NHL games. I think he would have done better if he had been more of a team player. As talented as he was, he didn't pass the puck much.

Management asked me to be an assistant coach as well as a player, but I didn't want the responsibility. I knew it was my last season playing hockey and I just wanted to have fun. I helped Bryon a little, ironing out the wrinkles in our power play and that kind of thing, but I didn't make much of a contribution otherwise. I finished sixth in team scoring with 21 goals and 50 points. My age played a role in my declining performance and so did my drinking. My agent shopped me around to some NHL clubs, hoping one would take a chance on me, but none would.

NEEDLESS TO SAY, I wasn't in a good headspace when Isabel and the kids came to visit for a weekend. It was impossible to ignore the huge cracks in our marriage. After a day or two, it was clear the relationship couldn't continue. Isabel took the kids and headed back to New Jersey. My marriage was over for good. I had known the end was coming but I was devastated anyway.

THE MONTANA MAGIC didn't generate much interest and the club struggled financially. It got so bad that six players refused to lace up for a game against the Colorado Flames in March because they hadn't been paid. I wasn't being paid regularly either, and unfortunately, the funds from Ermineskin never materialized. I didn't boycott any games but I sure wasn't happy to be lacing up.

We won just 20 of 76 games that season and finished dead last in the five-team league. The Magic's first season turned out to be its last. It was also the last of twenty-one seasons for the CHL. It folded a month after the Tulsa Oilers won the championship. The league owned the team at that time because the owners had gone into receivership.

My professional hockey career was over. My life had revolved around the sport since I was kid. I had no formal education, no training in a trade, and absolutely no idea how I would spend the rest of my life. Between that and my collapsed marriage, I was at a complete loss. I couldn't cope with the situation so I tried to escape from it. I started drinking every day. I would sometimes drink to a point where I no longer felt drunk—and then I would start all over again.

Back in Philadelphia, I moved into the home of a friend named Larry Aronson. He was good enough to let me stay in the basement suite. Larry lived upstairs with his wife and two kids. My kids were living with their mother nearby, but I had little contact with them, mainly because I felt I had failed them.

In October, a friend helped get me a job selling cars at a Mitsubishi dealership. It was obvious from the start that I wasn't cut out for it. I wasn't at ease outside of hockey circles and I didn't feel comfortable making conversation, let alone a sales pitch.

I've always been a giving person, and that trait wasn't a job asset either. Instead of trying to get as much money as possible for a used car, I would tell the customer how much the vehicle was really worth and we would settle on that. I was working on commission, so I wasn't exactly raking in the money. The only thing I liked about that job was the company car I drove.

I would sometimes get together with the other salesmen after work, having a few drinks at a place across the street from the dealership. Once in a while we had some late nights but, somehow, I always managed to wake up for work the next day.

I quit that job in the spring and spent the next four months on what I described as a "golf tour." I lived in my camper and traveled around to various celebrity golf tournaments. I would play in three or four a week. There were so many of those tournaments in the area, I could have played every day. Some of these events were paid appearances but that wasn't their major appeal. I just enjoyed golfing, meeting a lot of great people in the Philadelphia area, and drinking with the guys.

At the end of August, I headed to Northern Ontario with some of my former Flyers teammates to play in a hockey tournament that doubled as a fundraiser. We boarded a bus in Philadelphia and settled in for twelve-hour road trip. We spent the entire time playing cards and drinking. Some of us were hammered by the time our driver pulled up to the Canada–U.S. border near Buffalo, New York. We thought we might get pulled over, but when the customs official realized who we were, he just waved us through. I guess he was either a Flyers fan or an overworked government employee who didn't feel like dealing with a busload of hockey players who had downed a little too much happy ale.

We rolled into North Bay that night and checked into the hotel. I couldn't tell you much more about that weekend because it was a crazy few days.

By the time we got back to Philadelphia in the middle of the week, I had been drinking for days. I should have gone home to recover but I met up with some other friends and continued drinking instead—one of many bad choices I made in those days.

I stumbled into bed late Friday night, the start of the Labor Day weekend, and I was a wreck when I woke up. I spent much of Saturday with my head in the toilet and I couldn't stop shaking. It was the first time alcohol had ever made me sick, and I knew something was very wrong.

That night, I called Dominic Carlino, a doctor I knew socially, and he told me to go to a nearby hospital where he worked. I checked in on Sunday morning and they ran a battery of tests on me. When Dominic walked into my room later that day, he took one look at me and said, "Rifle, you look like crap." He was right, of course. I knew him as a guy who was always kidding around, but that day he was deadly serious. "You have two choices," he said. "Either you stop drinking now or you keep drinking and you die."

He said he could get me help, but only if I really wanted it. He knew that I was feeling so sick at the time, I would have agreed to *anything* that might make me feel better, so he told me to take some time to think about it.

I spent much of that day lying in bed thinking about the role drinking had played in my life and about the toll it had taken on my career and my marriage. My life was spinning out of control. There was no denying it. I decided then and there that I would turn my life around. The following morning, I told Dominic I was ready for rehab. The next day, I checked into nearby Maryville Addiction Treatment Center.

Some people would describe those few days as the worst in my life, but I don't. I look back at that weekend as the best of my life because it was the start of the journey that led me to where I am today.

9

Rebirth

(1985–2007)

When I checked into the Maryville facility in Williamstown, New Jersey, I filled out a form of questions about my life and about my history with alcohol. When asked about the likelihood of me drinking after rehab, I said that would never happen. I wasn't being honest. I was just telling administrators what I thought they wanted to hear. Alcoholics lie to avoid facing the consequences of their actions. In time, they become such seasoned liars, they lie to themselves. No question, alcoholics are excellent con artists. This may be due to denial, shame, or a mix of both.

I was assigned a private room but I spent quite a bit of time with other patients. Men and women were segregated in terms of accommodations, but group sessions were mixed. We were from different backgrounds and walks of life but we all had similar painful stories, and we shared them in group counseling. Treatment was based on the guiding principles of the Alcoholics Anonymous twelve-step program, which stresses the importance of recognizing a higher power, relying on the support of family and friends, and remaking your life.

Through those sessions and one-on-one counseling, I was able to step back and take a good, hard look at my life. It was very difficult to look at my past. In just a few short years, I had left behind my life as a carefree kid to become a married father of two. I had gone from relative obscurity to hockey stardom—and life in the fast lane. The change had been overwhelming and I had turned to alcohol to help me cope. The counselors suggested that drinking had become my relief valve, a way to deal with the pressure of having to perform at a high level on the ice. It also became my way of dealing with the loss of my family and the end of my career. I was only thirty-five and felt I had lived several lifetimes already.

Life at Maryville was very structured. We woke up early in the morning, ate scheduled meals, exercised, and attended training and group sessions at set times. We were kept busy all day and were required to observe a strict curfew at night.

I learned a lot about myself while I was there and about the importance of making good choices. To change my life, I would have to change my daily routine and habits. If I didn't, I could relapse and end up in the same rut and on the same destructive path that I had been following.

Friends who visited me while I was in rehab understood the challenges I faced and they offered to be my support system when I completed the six-week program. I really appreciated that.

After a month in treatment I was in good physical health, and I started counting the days until I could go home. Before checking out, I filled out the same form I had been handed on my first day. What a difference six weeks can make! The questions were the same but all of my answers were different. When asked about the likelihood of me drinking after rehab, my answer was more thoughtful. I said I would be able to stay sober, but only if I was mindful of the lessons I had learned in rehab. I was finally being honest. Rehab was like preschool in a way; it was just the beginning of my road to recovery. I headed home in October 1985 determined to start a new life. I was confident I would succeed in doing that; when I made up my mind to do something, I did it.

I continued going to AA meetings after I left and that helped with my recovery. I felt awkward and slightly embarrassed at the first few meetings, but that didn't last long. I soon realized that we were all in the same boat, and there for the same reason—to overcome an addiction.

I MET WITH Billy and Clarkie for lunch a few weeks later. When conversation turned to hockey, they encouraged me to return to the ice. They suggested I play for the Hershey Bears, the Flyers' American Hockey League affiliate, with an eye to returning to the Flyers or possibly working as an assistant coach down the road.

The idea appealed to me a lot so I started skating on my own at one of the Flyers' practice facilities. I spent hours on the ice late at night, just as I had as a boy in Riverton. I was probably in the best shape I had been in for years. I still loved the feel of my skate blades cutting into the ice and the weight of the puck on my stick, but the more I trained, the more anxious I became.

It slowly dawned on me that I was about to return not just to the game I loved but also to the life of professional hockey player, a life that involved spending time in bars and other places where beer taps were open. I knew I had to avoid situations that would trigger a relapse in my drinking—so after a lot of thought about what I had just fought through and careful reflection on what I had learned, I decided not to make a comeback. Sure, I might have been able to stay sober in Hershey and even return to the NHL. I'll never know, but I have no regrets. I made a choice, one that was best for me at the time. I chose sobriety over professional hockey, and it was the best decision of my life.

A RECOVERING ALCOHOLIC needs help from others, and I had it in spades. While my drinking buddies disappeared when I gave up booze, my true friends stood by me. Former teammates, especially Orest Kindrachuk and Bob Dailey, supported me in my effort to remain sober. Whenever someone we met tried to persuade me to have "just one beer," one of the guys would pipe up on my behalf saying, "Let this one go. He doesn't drink." If not for my friends and the AA meetings I attended regularly, I might not have stayed clean those first few years after rehab.

AT THAT TIME, Rick MacLeish was selling insurance for a company owned by a friend. Ricky put me in touch with the guy, who offered me a job on the condition that I pass the licensing exam. I applied myself to my studies for the first time in my life and passed the exam on my first try. That gave me a great sense of accomplishment. I sold insurance for a year or two but I didn't like it much. As I said earlier, I wasn't a natural-born salesman. Also, I didn't like wearing a shirt and tie to work every day. I quit the job near the end of 1987, when a friend suggested I try landscaping.

The idea made perfect sense. I had spent childhood summers maintaining the Luprypas' golf course near Riverton, and I knew a lot about planting trees and shrubs, laying sod, doing stonework, performing lawn maintenance, and those kinds of things. So with the little money I had, I bought a little red

“**Reggie** was a great player but I think he made the right decision in not returning to hockey when he came out of rehab. That might have led to a backslide. He turned his life around and is making a big contribution to society now. I couldn't be more proud of him.”

BILL BARBER

Mitsubishi truck and two Lawn-Boy mowers, and started my own business. I called it "Sports Lawn Service." At first, my only clients were about a dozen friends and acquaintances. But my business expanded after a chance encounter at a celebrity golf tournament.

I was in a golf foursome with someone who worked at a property management company. When conversation turned to work, I told him about my little business and he told me his company managed public housing complexes. One thing led to another, and the company hired me to maintain the grounds at one medium-sized, ten-acre complex. The number of properties grew to five the following year and kept climbing.

Within five years, my business had grown to include the maintenance of twenty-five complexes, while the company's assets included twenty employees, a half-dozen vehicles, and about $500,000 worth of equipment. My company made about a million dollars in revenue annually.

I managed properties in North Jersey, South Jersey, the Philadelphia area, and Delaware. That required a lot of traveling. I would get up at 4 a.m., get my morning coffee, and drive to the site. I wouldn't return home until after 6 p.m. To me, running a business was like managing a hockey team. It required a lot of hard work and discipline. But in the landscaping business, I had the winters off instead of the summers.

Working in the projects could be quite an adventure. I witnessed drug deals, fights, stabbings, and worse. You name it, I saw it.

A few times, when we tried to adjust some recently laid sod that was out of place, we discovered bags of cocaine tucked underneath. They had been put there by drug dealers, so we didn't dare touch them. We just reported them to the building manager.

The projects were home to gang members, so robberies and even shootings were not uncommon. One of my employees and I were leaning against a building during a break at a property in North Jersey one day when a red car came around the bend and stopped about thirty feet from us. A passenger rolled down a tinted window and shot a guy standing on the curb. The poor guy took two bullets to his torso, which knocked him back about twenty feet against a fence. Remarkably, he got up and ran into a building. The victim was one of many tenants whom I had gotten to know while working there. We were rattled but we managed to collect our equipment and get the heck out of there. I later heard the guy survived that shooting, which was over drugs and a debt of $300. He was killed weeks later.

Another time, in Camden, New Jersey, we were putting up a retaining wall when we heard gunfire. We looked up and saw two groups of armed men. We ducked behind the wall and watched as they shot at each other while running past a building. They saw us but they didn't care; they were only interested in killing each other. When they disappeared around a corner, I turned to my employees and said, "Okay, guys, time to leave!" None of the bad guys got hit. I guess they were all really bad shots.

We didn't talk to police about either of those incidents. One thing you learn while working in the projects is that you keep your mouth shut or risk losing your life. Another thing you learn is to be aware of your surroundings at all times. Even today, I am always aware of everything that is going on around me.

Despite the risks of working in the projects, I enjoyed it. Though you had to be wary of a very small percentage of the residents, most of them were wonderful. They all had tough lives so I helped them out when I could. I used to hire them to do weeding or plant flowers for a few hours or a day, and sometimes created small jobs for them even when I didn't need help.

I got to know some of the families quite well, and at Christmas, I would buy them food for their holiday dinners and presents for their kids. One kid in particular sticks out in my mind. I saw him grow from a toddler into a young man over the twenty-year period I operated my business in that area. He sold drugs and was always in and out of jail. He used to let me know when he was headed to the clink. "Mr. Leach," he would say, "I'm off to Disney World again." Once, when a blower was stolen from the back of my truck, he said he would look into it—and the equipment reappeared an hour later.

Many of the other people I got to know also protected me. For example, if a guy from another complex gave me hard time, one of the residents would step in and tell him to back off.

It just goes to show, if you treat people well, they will treat you well.

Eventually, I decided that managing a sizeable business was more of a hassle than it was worth. Too much money was going out to pay employees, pay insurance, and repair and buy equipment, and not enough was coming in. I downsized to the point where I maintained just nine properties on my own with help from temporary workers. I also subcontracted tree work, concrete sidewalks, and wrought iron fencing. The business was more manageable and I took home more pay.

WHILE MY LANDSCAPING business was thriving, my personal life was improving. After a period of being estranged from Isabel and the kids, I mended relations with them and, although I lived separately from them, I was still a part of their lives. I called Isabel once in a while to see how she was doing. I can't say enough good things about Isabel. I may not have been the best husband, but she put up with me for years and was always concerned about my well-being even after we split. I don't know how she managed to forgive me, but I'm grateful she has. I enjoy my time with her and I get a kick out of her partner Mark Stevens, a member of the legendary doo-wop singing group The Dovells. We joke a lot with each other. I am also still very close to Isabel's family, whom I care for deeply and who have always accepted me.

I also began spending time with Jamie and Brandie, and today, my bond with my children is stronger than ever. Jamie had been passionate about hockey all his life. He had carried around a miniature stick as a toddler—we could never pry it out of his hands—and later spent time on the ice with me and my teammates after Flyers practices. He rose through the ranks of minor hockey as a solid two-way player. I give all of the credit to Isabel, who ferried him to and from hundreds of games and 6 a.m. practices over the years, sometimes driving an hour and fifteen minutes each way.

When Jamie was sixteen, he moved to British Columbia to play for the New Westminster Bruins of the Western Hockey League. Mark Recchi was one of his teammates. I had encouraged Jamie to join the team because the coach was none other than Paddy Ginnell. He was a great coach who had played a pivotal role in my career. I knew he would be able to help Jamie advance in his own career. Unfortunately, Paddy got fired a couple of months after Jamie arrived.

From there, Jamie went to the Ontario Hockey League, where he played for the Hamilton Steelhawks and then the Niagara Falls Thunder. In 1987, the Pittsburgh Penguins picked him in the third round of the entry draft. Any father would be pleased to have his son follow in his footsteps, and that was certainly true for me.

A buddy and I drove seven hours to watch Jamie play in his first NHL game. I felt incredible pride watching my son step onto the ice in Pittsburgh that night wearing the same jersey as Mario Lemieux and Paul Coffey. I have to admit, I also felt a little old realizing how much time had passed. It seemed to me that I had been in the NHL just a short time before and Jamie was only a toddler, yet here I was watching my son turn pro.

Jamie ended up playing parts of five seasons in the NHL, including two in which the Penguins won the Stanley Cup. He skated for the Canadian junior national team and played in an elite league in Britain. He also won the Calder Cup, which was the American Hockey League championship, as part of the Rochester Americans. He won three Allan Cups, awarded annually to the senior amateur men's champions of Canada. That gives him more championship rings than me. Jamie went on to coach junior hockey for two years. He won the title of Coach of the Year in the Manitoba Junior Hockey League, and he later became a golf pro.

Jamie, who now lives in Winnipeg, touches base with me a couple of times a week, and I love spending time with him, his wife, Shannon, and their son, Jaxon. Shannon gives great hugs and we are able to joke with each other quite a bit. She is a very smart lady and a playful mother to Jaxon. Jaxon, my youngest grandchild, who shares my birthday and is my greatest birthday gift, has been skating since he was about three years old. Every winter, Jamie builds an outdoor rink in their backyard, which isn't hard to do in Winnipeg. In weather so cold that most of us cannot stand it, Jaxon fusses when asked to come inside because he wants to keep skating.

Brandie was also a very good athlete. After graduating from Cherry Hill High School in New Jersey, Brandie enrolled at the University of Manitoba to study science. She also made the Canadian lacrosse team, and I flew to Scotland to watch her play in the 1993 World Cup. I didn't tell her in advance, so she was shocked when the middle-aged man who approached her on the sidelines hiding behind a video camera turned out to be me. Brandie was one of the youngest women on the national team but she more than held her own, and watching her play was another proud moment for me.

Today, Brandie lives in Texas, where she and her husband, Chris, both chiropractors, run a clinic specializing in sports services. Brandie and I have always been very close—our personalities are very similar. We speak two or three times a week and visit each other often, even though we live far apart. Brandie also coaches the University of Texas women's lacrosse team. She has been recognized as the Coach of the Year twice in their national league. Her husband, Chris, is the best son-in-law you could ask for. He and I have an ongoing competition on the golf course. I just love him and being around him. I am happy to have him as my other son. Their children, Jaden and Hunter, are a great source of joy to me.

Both Jaden and Hunter are very athletic. Jaden, my oldest grandchild, has a beautiful singing voice and is an entrepreneur already. At the age of ten, she owns a jewelry franchise. She excels at all sports, and tennis is currently her game of choice. Hunter is a lot like me in his goofy demeanor and good sense of humor. He loves playing football and basketball, but his passion is playing the greatest game on earth, hockey. I always say that now I have to live at least another twenty years to watch my grandchildren's accomplishments!

To date, three members of the Leach family have represented Canada in international competition. Because I wore the number 28 when I skated for Team Canada, Jamie chose the same number when he played for the World Juniors—Brandie also wore 28 for the Canadian Women's Lacrosse Team. Brandie has all three of our jerseys with that number.

About two years after my trip to Scotland to surprise Brandie, I married a woman I had met while skating in a Flyers' alumni hockey game. Debbie had two sons, Rudy and Brandon, and I became close to them. I also became very close to her parents, especially her father, Albert. He and I watched more than a few horse races together. Debbie and I had our ups and downs, like any married couple, but we eventually started having more bad days than good and we parted ways in 2005. I'm still in touch with both kids, whom I consider family. Debbie also keeps me posted on what's going on with the boys. Even though the marriage didn't work out, I have no regrets. Everyone who has been part of my life has played a role in helping me along my life's path. I believe every person who has come into my life has done so for a reason or as a teaching, helping me learn valuable life lessons that I am now obligated to share.

AROUND THAT TIME, I became more interested in charity work, which spurred me to support many fundraisers and charitable events over the years. For eight years, I hosted an annual celebrity golf tournament that raised money for cancer research. At each of those events, there would be a celebrity in each foursome. We raised about $150,000 every year.

Professional athletes are always taking from the community—fans buy game tickets and paraphernalia, and businesses give us cars and other freebies—so I think we should give back.

A lot of athletes do, which is why it was easy for me to recruit so many of them to play in those tournaments.

Dozens of famous athletes took part in my tournament over the years, and not just from the world of hockey. Philadelphia Eagles quarterback Ron Jaworski teed off, and so did Vince Papale, the Eagles wide receiver whose incredible story—he was thirty years old when he made his NFL debut—was the basis for the movie *Invincible*. NBA star Charles Barkley also came out. He was a first-rate power forward but possibly the world's worst golfer.

WHEN THE FLYERS were the toast of the town, athletes, politicians, movie stars, and other celebrities wanted to meet us. I chatted with everyone from Sylvester Stallone to Ted Kennedy and Muhammad Ali. Baseball player Tug McGraw, Tim's father, was also a great friend. The Flyers of our era always had front-row seats and backstage passes to every event, professional league game, and concert in Philly. I was there when the Flyers presented vertically challenged comedian Don Rickles with a jersey that had the number "½" on the back. It seemed odd for me to be signing autographs for the likes of professional golfers Payne Stewart and Phil Mickelson. It always threw me for a loop when someone I admired from the celebrity world recognized me and wanted to talk. It still does.

We were once walking through the lobby of a Los Angeles hotel when we met the cast of the television show *Charlie's Angels*. The women were as beautiful as you would expect. They all knew who we were, and Cheryl Ladd turned out to be a hockey fan and really friendly. Joe Kadlec invited them to our game against the Kings but they made an excuse and politely declined—not surprising as our rowdy reputation likely preceded us.

We also ran into *Three's Company* star Suzanne Somers at the airport in Vancouver. She knew who we were because we had already met her husband, Canadian entertainer Alan Hamel. She was beautiful and friendly, and I was a fan of her show.

AFTER MY MARRIAGE to Debbie ended, I started thinking about making a change. Also motivating me was the fact that my kids were worried about me working in the tough areas in the Delaware Valley. I was considering my options and the possibility of moving back to Canada when I was invited to attend the 2007 Little Native Hockey League tournament in Northern Ontario.

One of the biggest minor hockey tournaments in Canada, it includes more than 170 teams from across Ontario. All the players are First Nations boys and girls aged four to seventeen. For more than four decades, the tournament has been a big event in Aboriginal community and a chance for First Nations people to get together. It is also a great skill showcase for up-and-coming hockey talent and has produced some well-known Aboriginal NHL players. Jonathan Cheechoo, Stan Jonathan, Ted Nolan along with his sons, Brandon and Jordan, and Chris Simon all played in this tourney as kids.

I flew up to Sudbury, Ontario, for the tournament, and it was a weekend that ended up changing my life.

10

Full Circle

(2007–PRESENT)

WHEN I ARRIVED in Sudbury, I met with the tournament organizers. One of them was a beautiful woman who was selling raffle tickets. I bought a ticket from her, telling her I felt good about my chances. When I didn't win, I walked up to her and, pretending to be upset, threw my ticket on the floor. My attempt at humor was a complete flop. She just said, "Sorry you didn't win, but you contributed to a good cause." Then she walked away, probably in disgust. That is how I first met Dawn.

At the time, she didn't recognize me as their invited guest, and later, when the event organizers asked her to join us for dinner, she looked directly at me and declined. It was no coincidence that Dawn and I had spent a lot of time working together during that tournament, handing out medals and trophies. We found out later that the other coordinators had planned it that way, knowing we were both single. But as you know, I work hard to achieve my goals—and my goal was to get to know her. Between our tournament responsibilities, we started to chat. It took some time and dozens of long-distance phone calls over the next few months, but she finally warmed up to me.

We started dating after I invited her to one of my alumni events in Toronto.

We began sharing our worlds with each other. I told her about hockey and Philadelphia, and she opened up about her involvement in powwows and First Nation communities. Having five brothers, she had always been around hockey, and she knew the game fairly well.

It turns out we had many friends in common from across Canada. It's a small world. At an Aboriginal festival in Winnipeg where I was a guest, I introduced Dawn to my son Jamie and his wife, Shannon. We all had a great time.

Not long after that, I was invited to Isabel's birthday party in New Jersey. I invited Dawn to join me at the celebration to meet my family, friends, and hockey brothers.

Isabel and the kids liked Dawn the instant they met her, and it's not hard to understand why. She is a pillar of the community and a tireless advocate for First Nation people—Dawn helps create business and economic opportunities for First Nation and Aboriginal people across Canada—and also a loving mother to her daughter, Crystal. Like me, she is also from a large family. Dawn is an exceptional woman who has brought much love to my life.

We knew we had something special, so in November 2007, I moved to her community on Manitoulin Island, in Northern Ontario. It was the first time I had ever lived in a First Nation community. I loved it there, and I still do. Located in the north end of Lake Huron, Manitoulin is the world's largest freshwater island. With its clear waters, great fishing, and outstanding natural scenery, it seemed like paradise to me.

Aundeck Omni Kaning First Nation couldn't be more different from Philadelphia. It's a tiny community on the north shore of the island and life there is quiet—very quiet. There are no expressways or shopping malls, and you can't even order pizza delivery on a Friday night. The only traffic lights around are the ones at the swing bridge that connects the island to the mainland. In my first few months here, I felt like I had moved to another planet.

But the natural beauty of this island and the slower pace make it an ideal place to live. About half of the population is First Nation and all of the people here, Aboriginal and non-Aboriginal alike, have treated me well, making me feel welcome.

As challenging as the change was early on, I didn't regret it. I was glad to be sharing a life with Dawn. Now that we are married, I am happy to say she is a devoted wife to a guy who is a little rough around the edges, and sometimes a little worse for the wear, but our common Ojibwe heritage and large family background strengthened our bond. Through her, I became more connected to my roots and to the Aboriginal community.

I started going to powwows, celebrations that showcase Aboriginal music, dance, food, and crafts. I love watching the beautiful young women performing in their jingle dresses, fancy shawls, and traditional outfits. The men dance too, in various dance styles such as traditional, grass, and fancy bustle, but I can't join them. My feet just don't move that way. Still, Dawn keeps instructing me on how to dance from a power skating position.

Coming from a large family herself, Dawn is very family-oriented, strongly supporting and encouraging my involvement with family. We get together several times a year with my kids, the grandkids, Isabel, and Mark. Dawn and I recently took the grandkids to Disney World for the trip of a lifetime and had a lot of fun—but boy, did they run us ragged. Keeping up with Bill Barber on an odd-man rush was never as tough as keeping up with my grandson Hunter on a mad dash to a ride in the Magic Kingdom.

"Through my travels with Reggie, I have learned that he has a positive impact on people. I have seen how Elders slowly approach him, somewhat starstruck, and then grab ahold of his hand. They tell him about how much enjoyment and pride he brought to them 'when hockey was real hockey.' Then I see how children he met at hockey schools or tournaments come running into his arms with big smiles and ask him if he will watch their games. Reggie will then make it a point to go to their games and visit with them again after the game to let them know how well they played. But what is most compelling is the many people who come to me and tearfully confide that Reggie has virtually saved their lives. He has coached them into sobriety. I get to witness this amazing human being who has bought winter jackets for kids in need, who has given financial help to moms struggling to make ends meet, who has given gas money to guys going to try out for a hockey team, among other acts of kindness. He loves to give. And he is always conjuring up the next fundraiser plan for the next cause. When he gets that sparkle in his eye as another fundraising idea pops into his head, I know I will be 'volunteered.' So I have to be ready for the ride and hold onto my hat!"

DAWN MADAHBEE LEACH

Often our family get-togethers involve skating. How lucky am I to be able to skate with my grandkids Jaden, Hunter, and Jaxon? At my age, they should be tying my skates for me! But it is still the other way around for now.

I also enjoy my time with Dawn's daughter, Crystal. She is a beautiful young lady and a hockey fanatic. I can tell you that I have never watched as much hockey as I do now since I moved to Canada, so Crystal and I have great conversations about the sport. We both admire the Montreal Canadiens' Carey Price, an incredible goalie and a proud member of the Aboriginal community.

I HAD HELPED raise money for cancer research while living in New Jersey, and I continued my contributions in that area after moving to Manitoulin Island. Dawn and I hold fundraisers and golf tournaments to raise money for numerous causes, including cancer research, medical equipment, toys for children, and minor hockey. I am happy to get involved in almost any fundraising event. I put on a Santa suit for many of the local children's events during the holiday season. Nowadays, I don't need much padding to get that roly-poly look!

One of the most fulfilling activities of my life these days is visiting First Nation communities. I travel to about a dozen of them every year for speaking engagements and guest appearance across the country. First Nation people have come a long way in recent years but still have a way to go to fulfill our potential as individuals and as communities. There are a growing number of successful and progressive First Nations in Canada that are involved in the business world. I would love to see people on various reserves working together more closely and more often to improve the lives of our people as a whole. I believe that we really need to focus on the youth. Their voices and opinions need to be heard for the community to progress. I think that leadership training should be organized to share knowledge now with our future leaders. To overcome poverty, stronger supports need to be in place so that kids finish their schooling. Kids who are sent outside the community for higher education need to know they have community support —maybe through social media—to encourage them to stay in school. Perhaps we could motivate them by offering assistance in sports, music, or some other area if they pursue their studies. We also need to give kids with learning disabilities the help they need to thrive. The bottom line is that education is the only sure way out of poverty.

When I travel to different Aboriginal communities, I usually spend a day or two in each and meet their leaders, then join them at a special banquet, which we call a feast. At some point during the festivities, I stand up and give the keynote address. I prefer not to stand on a stage because I don't consider myself to be above anyone else. They generally ask me to speak about my hockey career. When first I started public speaking, I was awkward and I read directly from a script. But I no longer do that, and I'm much better for it. I speak from the heart, and that is really the only way to connect with people. I'm much more comfortable in front of an audience now.

Usually, on the second day of my visit, I stop by the local school and talk to the kids either in separate classrooms or all together in the auditorium. I tell them about my life, past and present, and I'm honest about my battle with alcoholism. I emphasize the importance of making the right choices in life, which means staying in school and staying away from drugs and alcohol. I urge the kids to take responsibility for the choices they make and not blame others for their problems. I want them to learn from my mistakes and I encourage them to phone or email me anytime if they need someone to talk to. Some kids have actually contacted me, and as a result I now have many lifelong friends who are trying their best to walk the right path.

Some of those visits have been very memorable. On a trip to a Métis community in Gillam, Manitoba, in 2013, I spoke to a group of about three hundred kids. I asked for a volunteer to be the "keeper of the ring"—the student who would be responsible for taking care of my Stanley Cup ring and showing it to the others. I said the volunteer would be required to give a short performance of some sort. A bunch of kids put up their hands. One boy caught my attention because he was bigger than the others. When I selected him, he stood up and sang "O Canada." He was a little uncertain when he started, but he gained confidence when the other kids joined in, and he ended the anthem singing in a strong, clear voice. It was great moment.

I spoke to the kids for more than an hour. They listened as I shared my story and they peppered me with questions. Like kids in every school I visit, they wanted to know what it was like to play in the NHL, how it felt to win the Stanley Cup, and all that. When one kid asked me how much the championship ring is worth, I gave my standard reply: the ring represents years of dedication and sacrifice on my part, so it's priceless and I wouldn't sell it for any amount of money. Another kid asked me the question that makes me laugh whenever I'm asked. He wanted to know if I had played hockey with Carey Price or Sidney Crosby. I gave my patented answer, "Look at me! I'm a wrinkled old man. Do you think those guys were around when I was in the NHL?"

"About four years ago, I invited Reggie to speak to the kids at schools in our area. He came out in September and I took him to ten schools in five days. It turned out to be an awesome experience. The principals and teachers were as excited to see him as the students. He made an impression on all the kids, especially one ten-year-old boy. Reggie's talk convinced him to pursue his dream of becoming an RCMP officer. He's now working hard in high school and planning to study criminology in university. That would make him the first person in his family to finish high school and get a post-secondary education. Reggie has a lot to do with that."

DARRELL WILLIER, First Nations, Métis and Inuit Education Coordinator, Peace Wapiti School Division, Grand Prairie, Alberta

The kids gave me a standing ovation when I finished my talk, which was wonderful. I then posed for pictures and signed autographs while the "keeper of the ring" showed off the gold hardware. Most of the kids gave me a hug on their way out. Later on, the principal informed me that the boy I'd picked to safeguard the ring was struggling academically and had trouble keeping up in class. At that moment, I realized the other kids had sung along with him as a show of support, and that really moved me.

One of my other memorable experiences came many years before that, on one of my first ever visits to a reserve. My message about substance abuse made an impression on one student, who approached me after my talk and asked for my help. She confessed to having a drinking problem, and even told me she was drunk at that moment. I knew she was being honest because I could smell the alcohol on her. During the conversation that followed she said she had no one to turn to for help. She said her parents were alcoholics and she didn't trust any other authority figures to be discreet. I promised to get her some help.

I went to the health center on the reserve that day and told them the story. The guy behind the desk said something along the lines of "We'll get to it later." I wasn't pleased. The girl had finally mustered the courage to reach out. We had a window of opportunity to help her and we had to act fast. I urged the community to provide her with help that day and, fortunately, they did. She went into rehabilitation and has been sober for the past twenty years. She kept in touch with me for quite a while afterwards.

Sometimes when I am presenting at a community feast, I will direct my comments to parents, since they are the first teachers kids have, especially when it comes to learning kindness, respect, and love. Many parents and grandparents have struggled with maintaining these values themselves due to the trauma they and others went through in Indian residential schools. They were taken from their communities as young children, and the stories of the various kinds of abuse they experienced are heartbreaking. Their trauma has echoed through several generations of First Nation people. They didn't get to learn about kindness and love from family. But I remind the parents that they still have choices, and that choosing to teach these strong values to the kids helps them live a better life.

I MENTOR YOUNG people on the ice, too. Within a few months of moving to Canada, I was asked to get involved with the Manitoulin Islanders, a Junior A team in the Northern Ontario Junior Hockey League (NOJHL). The team was in rough shape when I took over, and despite my efforts over two seasons, the first as head coach and the second as head coach and general manager, the team's standing didn't improve.

Manitoulin didn't have a strong enough economy to provide the financial backing we needed to properly ice a traveling team. Plus we had difficulty attracting players as we didn't have the services or post-secondary schools that the larger towns or cities could offer. I can tell you that the club officials and a handful of volunteers fundraised like crazy to keep the team afloat. I never flipped so many burgers in my whole life as I did during that time at our many fundraisers. While I did have a contract with the team, I decided to forgo my salary, and even covered some of the expenses out of my own pocket. Many of the players did not have pocket money either, so I helped them along where I could. It was hard to concentrate on coaching when the team's financial situation was on my mind.

Just before I became involved with the team, one of the club's board members had put up her house as security for a line of credit for the team. But with the growing debt and no means to pay down that line of credit, we made the decision to sell the team. It was a difficult decision because we all loved hockey, but with our declining sponsorships and fan base, we had no other choice.

I would have loved to continue coaching that team. To this day, some of the guys keep in touch. (In fact, Dawn and I consider Mike Duffy, an import from New York who was the last team captain for the Manitoulin Islanders, our "adopted" son.) Many of them have gone on to become professionals in other fields, and I am really proud of them. When I was coaching, I spoke to some of them about life choices, just as Siggi had done with me years before. I'm not sure if I got through to anyone, but I know that some of them could have played at the minor professional level if they had tried.

In fact, there was one kid on our team, a young man from Texas, who was very dedicated. Mason Cossette showed up for every practice and game, and gave his all every time he stepped on the ice. He wasn't the greatest player on the ice when he started, but I added him to the roster because he had an all-star attitude. I believe commitment is more important than raw talent, and Mason is proof of that. He worked tirelessly on his skills and ended up playing minor pro hockey in the U.S.—and he's still playing today.

I'M NO LONGER involved in coaching at the junior level, but I still spend a lot of time on the ice, much of it with my son.

When Jamie finished his hockey career, he coached a few hockey teams and then became a golf pro. He loved working with kids and came up with the idea to start a hockey school. I got involved right away, seeing it as a way to help Aboriginal kids and their communities. Hockey plays a central role in First Nations communities, maybe even more than in other places. It connects isolated First Nations, showcases young local stars, and keeps kids busy and out of trouble.

A reserve typically sends five or six kids to a hockey school located somewhere else, sometimes thousands of miles away. When Jamie did some number crunching, he realized that, for the same cost as sending the kids away, we could run a hockey school on each reserve and provide instruction for all the kids, rather than just a handful. Reserves were receptive to the idea.

One of our first camps was held on Sheshatshiu Innu First Nation in Labrador. We flew into Happy Valley–Goose Bay, Newfoundland, on Christmas Day 2007, and spent the night at a hotel. A guy picked us up the next morning and drove us to the Innu community. I stared out the window in amazement for the entire fifty-minute drive. I had never seen so much snow in my life, not even during the harshest winters in Manitoba. It was piled so high on both sides of the road, I felt like we were driving through a tunnel. When we arrived in the community, which was very remote, we were pleasantly surprised to discover the local arena was modern and the ice was top notch. About ninety kids attended the school and they were so enthusiastic, I loved every minute with them.

During this same trip, our host took Jamie and me out on the land to visit a couple in their nineties who lived in what I would describe as a prospector's tent. Despite the cold, the temperature inside was really comfortable as they had a box stove in the

"My relationship with my father used to be strained. He was hard on me at times and he was very moody. You were never sure which guy you were going to get. But he has changed. He is happy now, much more positive and upbeat. The instructors who work at our schools love spending time with him and so does my son, Jaxon. My father and I have a good father–son relationship now and we see each other regularly. It's great."

JAMIE LEACH

center of the tent. There was wild game—rabbits and muskrats—hanging inside thawing to prepare for skinning. The couple invited us to join them for rabbit stew, biscuits, and Labrador tea. It was actually really good. Our camps allow Jamie and me to see some interesting places, particularly in the Arctic, and we get to taste amazing traditional foods everywhere we go. We also learn local customs. In Cambridge Bay, Nunavut, when we asked the Inuit kids a question, they weren't answering. When we asked our host about this, he said they were in fact responding. When they blink their eyes, that means "no," and when they open their eyes really wide, that means "yes." It sure helped us to know this to determine whether or not they were understanding the skating lessons!

When Jamie started the hockey school, he decided to name it Shoot to Score Hockey. I didn't find out until later that he chose that business name based on the advice I gave him as a youngster. I told him that when he shot the puck, he should always shoot to score. He owns the hockey school and I just help him where I can. We hold day camps, and not just on reserves, but also in dozens of other communities across Canada and the U.S. We offer several kinds of camps, ranging from those that focus on all-around skills to those where kids practice a specific skill like controlling the puck or shooting. We train nearly two thousand kids of all ages and levels every year. We have great instructors working with us, but Jamie or I make a point to be on the ice, too. I'm not sure how much longer that will last, but I'll be lacing up for as long as I can.

The kids at our camps spend time in the classroom, too. In those sessions, I deliver the same message I take into schools: try to make the right choices in life, and when you make bad ones, don't blame anyone else. Whatever choice you make, you own that choice, good or bad.

Because of my involvement with Jamie's school, a new generation of kids is getting to know me. I go to some of their games when they ask, and I always give the same feedback: keep both hands on the stick. The kids laugh because I say it so often in Shoot to Score sessions, I sound like a broken record. But really, how often do you see a young player scoring a goal with one hand on the stick?

When I think about my life today, I feel very fortunate that I still get to put my skates on and share my knowledge with these young hockey players.

NOW THAT I'M in the public eye in Canada, there has been a growing movement to get me inducted into the Hockey Hall of Fame. I still get a kick out of the grassroots movement to get me in. John K. Samson of the Weakerthans, an indie rock band from Winnipeg, composed a song calling for my induction and submitted a petition bearing about three thousand signatures to the Hall in 2013. The submission also included letters of support from several writers, including Joseph Boyden and Stephen Brunt. It's an honor to have such a passionate hockey fan in my corner, and I enjoyed surprising John on stage after one of his shows. There have been other petitions too, from other groups, efforts that really warm my heart. I may never be inducted, but that's okay. I have received so much support from Samson and many others that I feel like a Hall of Famer already. I tell people that they are my Hall of Fame. On a separate note, I should add that I'm proud of Billy Barber and Bobby Clarke for being in the Hall. They had to work a little harder than others to get there because they had me as a linemate!

Four decades after battling our way to the top of the NHL, the Broad Street Bullies are a tight group. Players and alumni from other teams often remark on the closeness that our team continues to share. Though I stayed away from hockey for several years after leaving rehab—I needed to make a fresh start in life—I reconnected with the Flyers organization in the 1990s. I now see my former teammates at Flyers alumni events and collector shows, and I keep in touch with some of them through email and phone. I consider Dave Schultz one of my closest friends today, and he often attends fundraising events I help organize. As you can imagine, the "Hammer" is always big draw. One of my most memorable experiences with the Flyers alumni was during the 2012 Winter Classic when I played again for the Flyers against the Rangers. I was on a line once again with Clarkie and Billy! The Flyers association had called on various players from each of the four decades of Flyers history to represent their team in this outdoor game in front of 45,000 fans. I was honored to play on a team with my former teammates and the younger guys like Mark Howe, Eric Lindros, Mark Recchi, Jeremy Roenick, and Brad Marsh against the likes of Mark Messier, Brian Leetch, Ron Duguay, and Glenn Anderson. The banter in the dressing room was just as funny, especially as some of the guys brought out the old equipment, liniment, and yards of bandage wrap. Bernie had his original goalie pads! We won 3–2 and had a blast.

Clarkie and I grew up together, and there is an unshakeable bond between us. No one except for us really knows the depth of the connection we have. From day one, we have understood one another. We have never judged each other, and we have always had each other's backs. Despite his sometimes tough exterior—he can be very blunt at times—he is very generous, a guy who takes care of others with absolutely no interest in being recognized for it. We don't see each other often, but when we get together it feels like no time has passed. Dawn says she is amazed at how little effort he and I put into catching up when we see each other as we carry on like we just saw each other yesterday. But Clarkie and I don't need to chit chat. We're like brothers to this day.

AS I HAVE come full circle in my life, reconnecting with family, I have learned more about my cultural heritage and strengthened my ties to the Aboriginal community. In 2008, I received a National Aboriginal Achievement Award, which is one of the highest honors that Aboriginal people in Canada can receive for recognition of their work. Several communities have also honored me with eagle feathers. Some of the feathers have been beaded with my name, my number (27), and the Flyers' colors. I have received gifts such as handmade beaded moccasins, mitts, and gloves. The beadwork I receive reminds me of my mother (grandmother) Kate, her beadwork, and all of the work that she did to raise me. She only saw me play a few times, but she did make it to Philadelphia to watch me and spend time with her grandchildren, and I'm thankful that she did. Later, when she had difficulty living on her own in Riverton, she moved into a long-term care home in Winnipeg. I visited her there often. Her mind was sharp and she could still remember the names of her many grandchildren, whose photos covered the walls in her room. In 1993, at age eighty-three, she passed into the Spirit World, but I believe she would be even more proud of the work that I do today than when I was a hockey player.

Two years later, in 1995, Archie passed away. He was ill with what was referred to as the black lung disease, common in miners. I visited him in the hospital in The Pas, Manitoba, before he passed. He had lived there with his wife and children. Our relationship was good and I still considered him more as my brother than my biological dad. He was always good to me and he expressed how proud he was of me, which was probably the closest we had come to being father and son.

Coming full circle, I have also spent more time with my Flyers brothers in recent years. Now we are all grandfathers. No matter where I am in life, I know I can call any one of them and pick up where we left off. We still reminisce, and the stories seem to be even funnier, or more exaggerated, now.

As I look forward to my years as a grandfather, I'm happy to be surrounded by my family, including my Flyers family. They've supported me, forgiven me, and made all my successes worthwhile. I don't know where I'd be without them.

I'VE LEARNED SOME traditional teachings of the Anishinabe (Ojibwe) people, basic values that every human being can live by. Most important to me are the Seven Grandfather Teachings—kind of appropriate to me, now, since I am a grandfather. Reflecting back on my journey, I see clearly how these teachings have been applicable to my life.

The Grandfather Teachings are Humility, Bravery, Truth, Honesty, Love, Respect, and Wisdom. I have learned that you can't achieve wisdom without realizing the other six teachings first. That makes sense to me.

When I think of the teaching of Humility, I reflect on growing up in a family of limited means. Despite that, my childhood in Riverton was wonderful. I received a lot of love and support, not just from my family but also from the entire community. Having been adopted as an infant by my grandparents was one of the best things that could have happened to me. I find it all very humbling.

I then consider the teaching of Bravery. I feel that if I had not taken my mentor Siggi Johnson's advice to leave my hometown at such a young age to pursue my dreams, I probably would not have made it to the NHL. Despite any natural talent I may have had, it is unlikely I would have followed the right path. I am forever thankful to Siggi for the guidance he gave me. It helped me make a brave choice.

I believe that everyone has a talent, skill, or gift in life. It is up to everyone to find that gift as your individual Truth. My gift was my hockey skills, which I sharpened every day through practice. But I think my incredible journey through life, one marked by dramatic highs and lows, has led me to the truth that I can help others. It is rewarding to know this gift still serves me today as I pass along my knowledge to young people.

The teaching of Honesty has allowed me to come to grips with my weaknesses. It was tough, but being brutally honest with myself is what saved me. I acknowledge that I have limitations and I respect them. I have been sober for thirty years.

I have learned real love through the forgiveness of my family. The teaching of Love has also shown me how to truly forgive myself and to welcome new love in my life. Out of love, Jessie put me in the care of my paternal grandparents, knowing they could provide me with a better life than she could. I'm grateful that I had the chance to spend time with her and Archie later in life. The love of my grandmother, Kate, will always carry me, as she was and always will be my mother.

One of the most important teachings I share with young people is Respect. Looking back, I can see times in my life when I didn't give other people the proper respect. Bob McCammon, my last coach with the Philadelphia Flyers, is one example. I ignored his efforts to motivate me and to help me perform at a higher level, and that was a mistake I still regret. He must have seen the same potential in me that I have since seen in the young men I coach.

After applying these first six teachings to my own life, I have been able to gain a level of Wisdom that allows me to live a life where I can give back and help others. First Nation youth, hockey buddies, and people from all walks of life contact me almost weekly asking for advice on how to deal with their challenges, their weaknesses, and their demons. I never hesitate to listen, offer advice if they ask, and take the necessary steps to assist them. I am there to help them follow through, as so many people were there to help me.

One of my sayings is "I never have any bad days, I only have some days that are better than others." When I really think about it, life is all about making choices. You can choose humility, bravery, truth, honesty, love, and respect. It's best to own your choices—don't blame others. Simply adopting the values of the Grandfather Teachings will make your life more enjoyable and meaningful. Some of the things I have learned I did the hard way, but I hope that my experience and my story will help others when they reach that fork in the road to choose the right path.

Acknowledgments

THIS BOOK WOULD not have been possible without the very kind support of many people.

The people of Riverton have always been a great source of support and pride for me, and I was honored to include their contributions in my story. Special thanks to Lloyd Roche, the family of Siggi Johnson, Eddie and the late Fred Luprypa's family, Carol Finnson, and Margaret Wisknowski, who supplied the history of our community and the highlighted the legacy of our Riverton Lions hockey team.

I'd like to acknowledge Ricky Reid and Keith Tomasson, who generously shared details of my time in Flin Flon, and to Darrell Willier, who spoke kindly about my speaking engagements at his schools.

To my linemates Bobby Clarke and Bill Barber, thank you for always being there for me. Dave Schultz, Bernie Parent, Ricky MacLeish, Orest Kindrachuk, Bob Dailey, Andre Dupont, Larry Goodenough, and all my Flyers brothers—you are an important part of my life story. I am also grateful to all the guys I've shared the ice with, who shaped my game and life—greats like Gordie Howe, Bobby Orr, Guy Lafleur, and Larry Robinson, as well as those from my junior and minor hockey days. Warm thanks to the important people behind the scenes: Cecile Baker, Joe Kadlec, and the rest of the crew who looked after us. Special thanks to Ed Snider, the Flyers Association, and the diehard Flyers fans for the great support over the years.

To my family: I hold each and every one of you close to my heart. It is my hope that this book will form an important part of our shared history. To my sisters Edna and Dorothy, my sincerest thanks for your unwavering support and your contributions to my story. To Isabel, thank you for your friendship, for being by my side during my hockey days, and for the gift of two great kids. To my son and daughter, Jamie and Brandie, I offer my deepest love and gratitude. Thank you for the blessings of the beautiful grandchildren—Jaden, Hunter, and Jaxon—that you have given me. They enrich my life immensely.

To my loving wife Dawn, thank you for the deep love we share and for walking beside me for each step of the journey in producing this book. It was always a dream of mine to tell my own story, and you helped make this dream come true.

Finally, I wish to acknowledge our friend Allan Clarke, who led Dawn and I to the whole team at Greystone Books, who have been a real pleasure to work with. Special thanks to publisher Rob Sanders, who is so gracious and accommodating. I'd also like to express my sincerest appreciation to Randi Druzin, my writer, and now friend, with whom I truly enjoyed "talking hockey."

Reggie Leach's Statistics

Season	Team	Games Played	Goals	Assists	Points	Awards & Championships
1970–71	Boston Bruins	23	2	4	6	
1971–72	Boston Bruins/ California Golden Seals	73	13	20	33	
1972–73	California Golden Seals	76	23	12	35	
1973–74	California Golden Seals	78	22	24	46	
1974–75	Philadelphia Flyers	80	45	33	78	Stanley Cup
1975–76	Philadelphia Flyers	80	61	30	91	Conn Smythe Trophy All-Star Game ('76)
1976–77	Philadelphia Flyers	77	32	14	46	
1977–78	Philadelphia Flyers	72	24	28	52	
1978–79	Philadelphia Flyers	76	34	20	54	
1979–80	Philadelphia Flyers	76	50	26	76	All-Star Game ('80)
1980–81	Philadelphia Flyers	79	34	36	70	
1981–82	Philadelphia Flyers	66	26	21	47	
1982–83	Detroit Red Wings	78	15	17	32